My Pretty
Brown Doll

My Pretty
Brown Doll

Crochet Patterns for
a Doll That Looks Like You

Yolonda Jordan

ABRAMS, NEW YORK

Table of Contents

Introduction   8

What You Need   12

Stitches & Techniques   18

Tips for Doll-Making   28

Base Doll

Base Doll Design   32

Hairstyles   50

Outfits

Basic Wardrobe   64

School Uniform   74

Collegiate Sweater   82

The Scientist   88

The Ballerina   96

Fairy Wings   101

Softball Uniform   104

Soccer Uniform   112

The Mermaid   120

Parisian Look   128

Resources   139

Acknowledgments   141

About the Author   142

Introduction

My great-aunt taught me to crochet when I was seven years old. Though I stopped crocheting for a long time because people kept telling me crochet was only for old ladies, I finally picked the craft back up in 2010. For almost three years I focused exclusively on making hats and scarves. Then in 2013, I made my first crochet doll.

Before making my first amigurumi doll, I googled "crochet dolls" and found myself scrolling through several pages of results before seeing an African American doll. I made a mental note of this, but to be honest I didn't think much about it. I already knew that my first doll would be made with brown yarn—a real reflection of myself. After finishing that first doll, whom I affectionately called Patience, I posted some photos on Instagram and Facebook. The response was overwhelming. So many people expressed how excited they were to see a doll that looked like them. Not too long after sharing Patience with the world, the custom requests started rolling in. I soon found myself with no time to make hats and scarves, as all my time was dedicated to perfecting a doll design. And so, My Pretty Brown Doll was born.

I specialize in crochet doll designs that embrace the pretty in every shade of brown. I aim to explore the art of crochet in a way that celebrates the magic of the African American experience. In addition to creating custom, one-of-a-kind doll designs, I am one of the first Black crochet designers to release a Black crochet doll pattern: my original Mia design.

And I'm so excited to share that design with you! Now you can create your very own doll, designed to look exactly like you or a special young person in your life. There is something so amazing about being able to create with your own two hands, to take yarn and a hook and make magic—Black Girl Magic, to be exact.

If you are new to amigurumi crochet-doll-making, you're in good company here. This book is structured to introduce you to the basics you'll need, and then to walk you step by step through all the instructions to ensure you can create the exact doll you want. And I've included plenty of special tips and tricks that I've learned over the years.

If you are a more experienced doll maker, you can skip ahead, and we will get this adventure started by first making a basic version of Mia. You can then decide what else you would like to make from there. Ballerina or soccer star? Scientist or fairy? Or maybe your doll can go seamlessly from school to soccer practice to the laboratory—it's all up to you and the lucky recipient of this doll!

The greatest part of this book is that you get to make a beautiful Black or Brown doll and have fun doing it. Whether you are making one for yourself or a loved one, it is my hope that when your doll design is finished, it is a reflection of all the magic there is, from hairstyle to eye color to the different outfits. So let's get started making your own Pretty Brown Doll!

What You Need

When you picked up this book, you probably knew that you would need yarn and a crochet hook, but there are a few more things that go into bringing your doll design to life. Some you may have thought of, and others may have you wondering how exactly they will be used. Below, I cover all the supplies you will need to complete the designs throughout this book.

Yarn

When choosing yarn, it is important to remember is that you are not just choosing the yarn that you will be using for the skin tone but also the yarns for the hair, outfit, and doll accessories. Synthetic worsted-weight yarn typically works best for the body of your design; however, I will not tell you to completely avoid natural fibers such as cotton because many yarn companies have produced natural-fiber yarns that will work really well. In creating the designs throughout this book, I did my best to stick with yarns that are easily accessible. You should be able to find most at the big-brand craft stores or online. See the Resources section (page 139) for a full breakdown of the yarns used for each design.

Crochet Hooks

If you are an experienced crocheter, you most likely already have a favorite crochet hook. If that is the case, make sure you have the right size crochet hook on hand. If you are still on the hunt for your favorite crochet hook, keep searching until you find the right one, because you will soon realize that your crochet hook is your new best friend. For the most part you will use the same size crochet hook for each design, but there are a few parts of the designs that may require you to use a smaller or larger hook. If this is the case, it will be noted in the pattern.

Safety Eyes

For the designs in this book, I only used one size of safety eyes: 15 mm. However, safety eyes come in many different sizes and colors. Changing the size and/or color of your eyes can change the look of your doll design. I recommend ordering your safety eyes online as they are not easy to find in stores. If you are not able to find safety eyes or prefer not to use them, you have the option to use buttons as eyes or even to embroider the eyes with yarn. Take note that if you do use safety eyes, they are permanent, so you want to be sure that they are positioned correctly and that they are the eyes you would like to use before securing them in place.

Stitch Markers

Right after your crochet hook, your stitch marker should be your other best friend. The cool thing about your stitch marker is that it can be super fancy, or it can be as simple as a strand of contrasting yarn. I personally use locking stitch markers because if I have to put my work to the side at any time, I am able to place the stitch marker in the loop of yarn and not worry about it unraveling. You can find stitch markers at most big-brand craft stores as well as online.

Stuffing

The stuffing is what is going to take your crochet from flat stitches to a beautiful doll design to put on display. I use 100 percent polyester fiberfill to stuff my designs. There are many different ways to stuff your designs, and you can use whatever method works best for you, but just be mindful that all stuffing is not created equal. I have found that polyester fiberfill, also known as "polyfill," works best for my doll designs, as it is lightweight and plush but will still allow the design to hold its shape.

Wooden Dowel

Think of the wooden dowel as your doll's spine. The dowel will keep your doll from having a floppy neck. I use ⅜-inch (1 cm) diameter × 12-inch- (30.5 cm) long dowels that are then cut down. The exact length that you need will be determined by the yarn used and your tension. You will need a handsaw or heavy-duty scissors to cut down the dowel.

Scissors

Be sure you have a good pair of scissors on hand. I recommend having two pairs. I have one pair specifically for cutting the yarn for my Afro Puffs and another pair for cutting yarn ends.

Yarn Needle

A needle that is slightly larger than a sewing needle, with a bigger eye for thicker fibers. You'll use a yarn needle to weave in ends.

Notions

Other items you can have on hand are a tape measure, buttons, craft felt, ribbon, beads, embroidery floss, craft glue, a pom-pom maker, hair ties or berets, a stitch counter—anything you can think of that you might want to try out on your doll design or that might make the doll-making process go smoother for you.

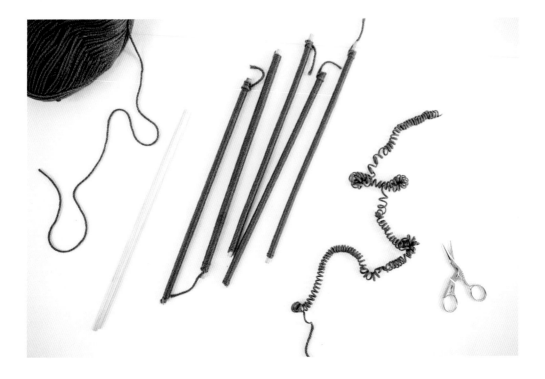

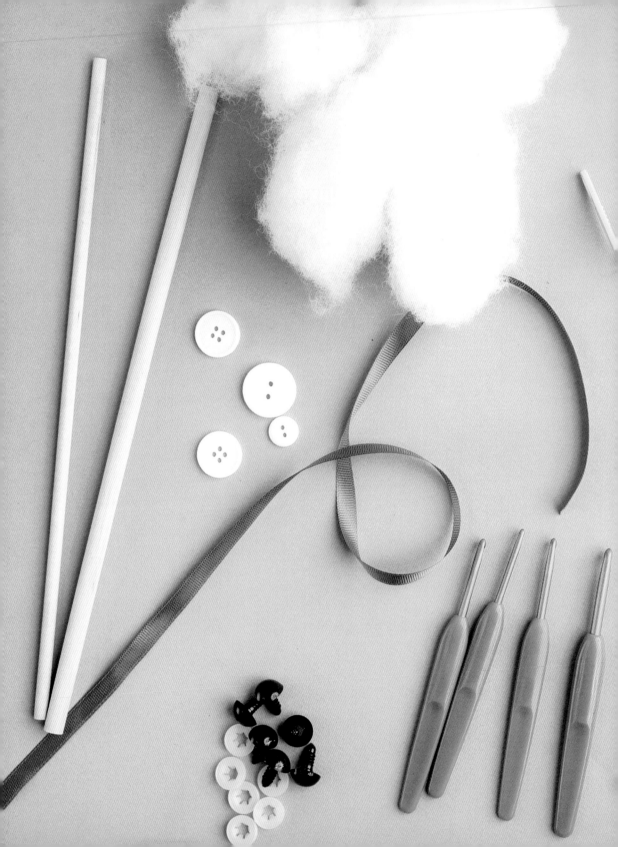

Stitches & Techniques

The term *stitch* in crochet refers to the shape achieved by moving your crochet hook through the yarn. In crochet patterns, it is abbreviated as st for a single stitch or sts for multiple stitches. You will notice that there is one stitch that you will use most often in your doll designs, and that is the single crochet (sc) stitch. The single crochet stitch is one of the most basic stitches in crochet, and it is perfect for doll-making because it is a short, stiff stitch that can be crocheted tightly—it's great for making plush dolls. Below are other terms and abbreviations you should be familiar with in your crochet doll-making journey.

Slip stitch (sl st)

The slip stitch is very similar to the chain; however, the slip stitch is normally used to join your work when working in the round or to get to another point in your project without using a noticeable stitch. To create the slip stitch, insert your hook into the top loops of the next stitch, yarn over, and pull through the loops of the stitch and the loop on your hook at the same time.

Chain (ch)

The chain stitch is created by first making a slipknot on your hook, then a yarn over, and then pulling the yarn through the loop on your hook.

Single Crochet (sc) (page 21, images 1–5)

To make the single crochet stitch, insert your hook into the stitch, yarn over, pull the yarn back through the stitch, yarn over, and pull through the two loops on the hook.

Double Crochet (dc)

I normally use the double crochet for clothing, particularly dresses or clothing that I want to be loose fitting. To make the double crochet stitch, yarn over and insert the hook into the stitch. Yarn over, pull the yarn back through the stitch, yarn over, and pull through the two loops on the hook. Yarn over and pull through the remaining two loops on the hook.

Half Double Crochet (hdc)

This is another stitch that I normally use for clothing. It allows me to work up the clothes a little faster and it does not have the stiffness of a single crochet. To make a half double crochet, yarn over and insert your hook into the stitch. Yarn over and pull the yarn back through the stitch, yarn over, and pull through the three loops on the hook.

Half Double Crochet Decrease (hdc dec)

Yarn over, insert hook into the first stitch, yarn over, pull up a loop, yarn over, insert the hook into the next stitch, yarn over, pull up a loop, yarn over, and pull through all loops on the hook.

Invisible Decrease (inv dec)

This is a great way to decrease your stitches in the round without leaving a hole or making the stitch bulky like a regular decrease. To make the invisible decrease, insert your hook into the front loop only of the next two stitches, yarn over, pull up a loop, yarn over, and pull through both loops on your hook.

Treble/Triple Crochet Stitch (tr)

The treble (or triple) crochet stitch is normally a stitch that I only use for clothing. It is rare to see this stitch in the body or base of a My Pretty Brown Doll design. To crochet the treble/triple crochet stitch, yarn over twice, insert your hook into the stitch, yarn over, pull up a loop, yarn over, pull through two loops on the hook, yarn over, and pull through all the loops on the hook.

Round(s) (Rnd[s]) (page 22, images 6–10)

The majority of your doll-making will be done in the round. In fact, you should be comfortable crocheting in a continuous round. That means you will not join the last stitch to the beginning stitch; you will simply continue crocheting around so there will be no recognizable beginning or end.

Magic Ring (page 23, images 11–20)

Most dolls are worked in continuous rounds. To start my rounds, I use the magic ring method. If you are familiar with other ways to work in the round, you can use those methods and still work the patterns in this book.

To create the magic ring, wrap the yarn around two fingers and create an X. Hold the X in place with your index finger and your thumb. Insert your hook into the loop on your two fingers from front to back, yarn over, and pull through the loop. Create a chain stitch to secure, and then crochet the number of single crochet stitches the pattern states. Once you have the beginning crochet stitches, you can pull the tail to close the ring.

Changing Colors or Adding in New Yarn

When you need to change colors, or if you happen to run out of yarn and need to add in yarn from a new skein, you can do so quickly with the two steps below.

1. Work your current stitch with the current yarn right up until the last step, just before you would make your last yarn over.
2. Drop your current yarn to the back and pick up the new yarn. Finish the stitch with the new yarn by yarning over with the new yarn and pulling it through the remaining loop(s) on the hook. To secure, continue working your stitches over the tails of the old and new yarns. After a few stitches (I normally make four or five), you can cut off the old yarn or previous color and continue working the pattern with the new yarn color.

Back Loop Only (BLO) and Front Loop Only (FLO) (page 24, images 21–23)

Normally you will crochet under both loops of a stitch, but occasionally you may need to only go into the back loop of a stitch or the front loop of a stitch. Doing so will allow you to create a little ridge in the front or the back of your work. In order to crochet into the back loop of the stitch, crochet the stitch as you would normally but only insert the hook into the back loop of the stitch instead of both loops. If the pattern says to go into the front loop only, crochet the stitch as you would normally but only insert the hook into the front loop of the stitch instead of both loops.

Finishing Off (page 25, images 24–25)

To fasten off, with hook still inserted in last stitch, cut yarn leaving a tail, yarn over, and pull tail through loop on hook. Using a yarn needle, weave in the tail.

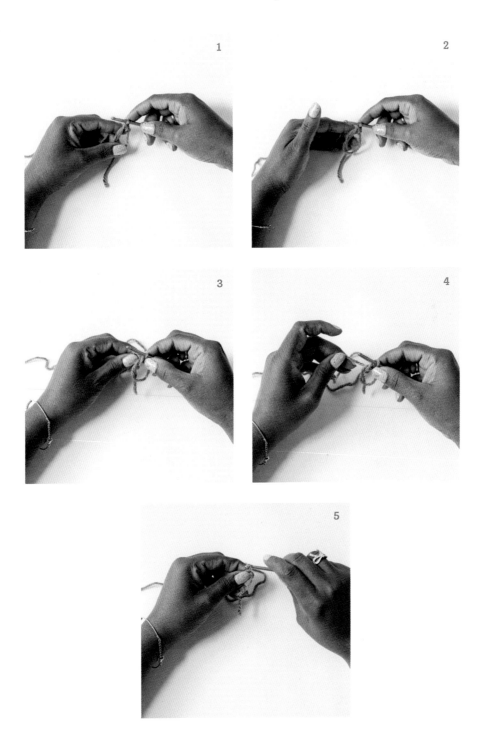

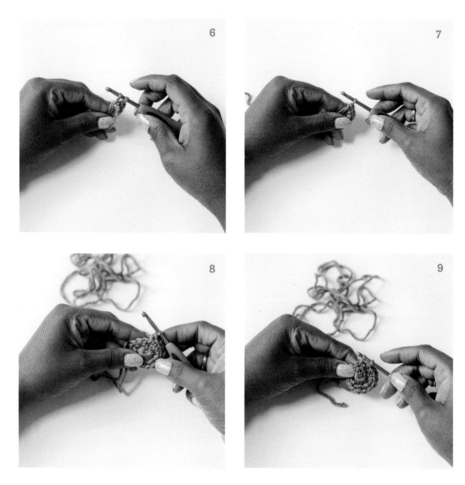

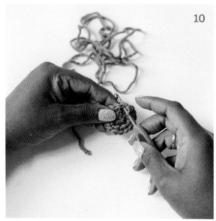

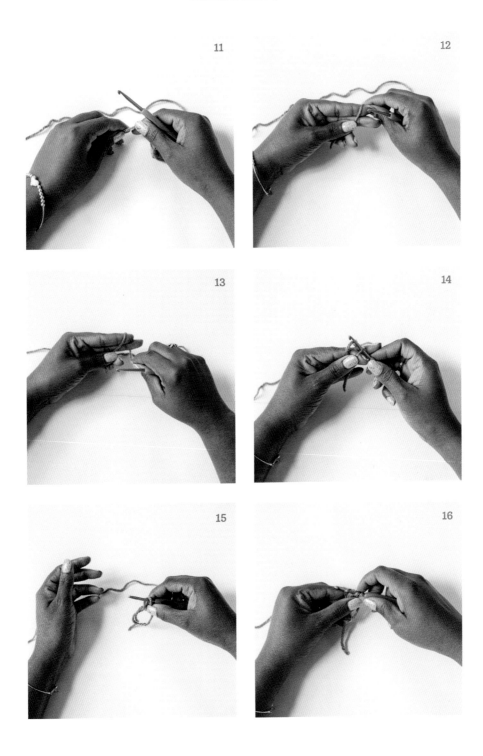

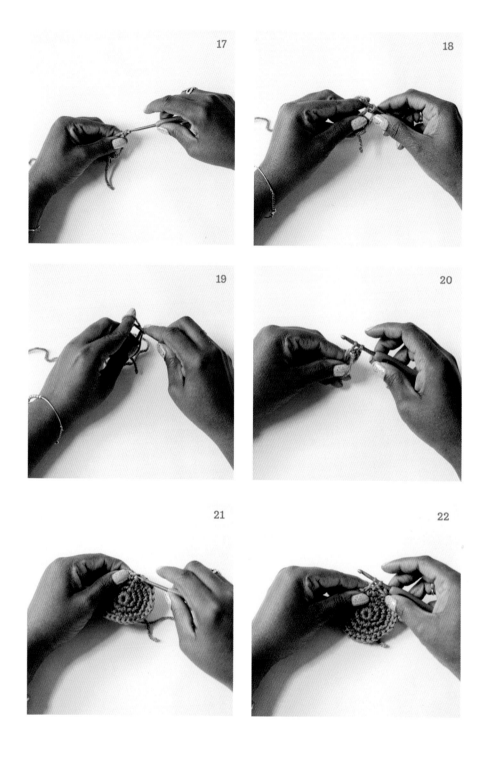

23

24

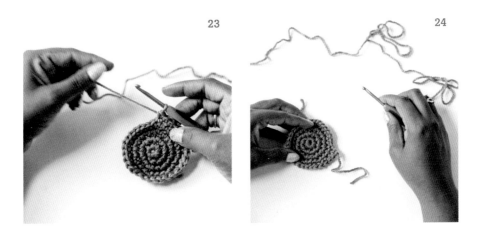

25

Tips for Doll-Making

Tension/Gauge

Be mindful of your tension. You want to have tight, even stitches, and the best way to achieve this is to finish a section of the doll design once you start. For example, try to finish the entire head of the doll once you start it, instead of starting and stopping. If you find that you do need to start and stop midway through, make sure that you are at a good stopping point and use a stitch marker to secure your stitches. You may also want to do a gauge swatch before you start to work on the entire design. This will help you decide if you need to use a smaller or larger hook than what is suggested in the pattern.

Stuffing

Be sure to stuff your design as you go. This will allow you to stuff firmly without overstuffing. If you wait until you have crocheted all the pieces to stuff, you may not be able to get the stuffing in all the small spaces. I use the end of my crochet hook or the wooden dowel to make sure I pack the stuffing in tightly. Stuff enough so that your doll is firm, but be careful not to overstuff. The stuffing should not be busting out of the stitches. If you can see a lot of your stuffing through your stitches, you are most likely overstuffing or your tension may be too loose.

Notes on the Patterns

Almost all My Pretty Brown Doll designs start with the head. You will find that for the most part, the head is done the same for each design. The adding of the additional facial features such as the eyes, nose, eyelashes, etc. are what will allow the personality of your design to shine through.

The designs throughout this book are what many in the doll-making world consider a leg-up doll design. This means that once you make the legs and connect them, the rest of the body is worked from the legs up. You are going to work the arms into the body, so once the legs and body are complete the only thing you will need to do is sew on the head.

At the end of each row or round of instructions is a number in parentheses. This is the stitch count—the total number of stitches at the end in that row or round. At the beginning of each round, place a stitch marker in the first stitch to help you keep count.

These tips will help you create a doll that you are super proud of. But, like with all things, practice makes perfect. The more you work on your doll designs, the more comfortable you will become with making them. Are you ready to get started? Now the fun begins! Let's get ready to make the base of the My Pretty Brown Doll design, Mia.

Base Doll

Base Doll Design

This base doll is inspired by one of my most-requested dolls to date. Mia is the first design I created with the two Afro Puffs hairstyle, and she was designed not only with me in mind, but with all the little African American girls who may have been told that they were not pretty or that the texture of their hair was not acceptable. Each design in this book is a modification of the Mia design, and you will find that by changing her outfit and hairstyle, you can bring a whole new doll to life.

~~~~~~~~~~~~~~~~~~~~~~~~~~~~~~~~~~

What You Need

Skin Tone: Approximately 185 yd (170 m) worsted-weight (4) yarn in the color of your choice. Yarn used is Red Heart Soft in the color Chocolate.

Underwear: Approximately 10 yd (9 m) worsted-weight (4) yarn in the color of your choice. Yarn used is I Love This Yarn in the color White.

Size US F/5 (3.75 mm) crochet hook

Or size needed to obtain gauge

Stitch marker

Yarn needle

Two 15-mm safety eyes

Polyester fiberfill

Small amount black yarn or embroidery thread for eyelashes and eyebrows (optional)

⅜-inch (1 cm) diameter × 12-inch- (30.5 cm) long dowel

Handsaw or strong scissors to cut the dowel

Finished Measurements

Approximately 15½ inches (39.5 cm) tall

Gauge

5-round circle = 2½ inches (6.4 cm) in sc using US F/5 (3.75 mm) hook

Pattern Notes

Work in continuous rounds. Use a stitch marker in the last stitch of the round to keep track of rounds.

At the end of a piece worked in the round, join with a slip stitch in the first stitch before you fasten off.

Head

Rnd 1: With skin-tone yarn, make a magic ring, 6 sc into ring, pull ring closed. (6 sc)

Rnd 2: 2 sc in each st around. (12 sc)

Rnd 3: *1 sc in next st, 2 sc in next st; repeat from * around. (18 sc)

Rnd 4: *1 sc in next 2 sts, 2 sc in next st; repeat from * around. (24 sc)

Rnd 5: *1 sc in next 3 sts, 2 sc in next st; repeat from * around. (30 sc)

Rnd 6: *1 sc in next 4 sts, 2 sc in next st; repeat from * around. (36 sc)

Rnd 7: *1 sc in next 5 sts, 2 sc in next st; repeat from * around. (42 sc)

Rnd 8: *1 sc in next 6 sts, 2 sc in next st; repeat from * around. (48 sc)

Rnd 9: *1 sc in next 7 sts, 2 sc in next st; repeat from * around. (54 sc)

Rnds 10–18: 1 sc in each st around.

Rnd 19: *1 sc in next 7 sts, inv dec in next 2 sts; repeat from * around. (48 sc)

Rnd 20: *1 sc in next 6 sts, inv dec in next 2 sts; repeat from * around. (42 sc)

Rnd 21: *1 sc in next 5 sts, inv dec in next 2 sts; repeat from * around. (36 sc)

Rnd 22: *1 sc in next 4 sts, inv dec in next 2 sts; repeat from * around. (30 sc)

Insert the safety eyes. I normally place eyes between Rnds 14–15 with approximately 5 to 6 sts between the eyes (images 1–2). After adding safety eyes, if you want your design to have lashes, embroider them now as follows: Using yarn needle and black worsted-weight yarn or embroidery thread, insert yarn needle from back to front at inner corner of eye, bring yarn up to curve over top of eye, insert yarn needle at outer corner of eye, bring needle up at approximately 1 stitch above, insert yarn needle into same stitch made at outer corner of eye (this should create your first lash), bring up yarn needle 1 stitch up and slightly over from previous stitch, insert yarn needle into same stitch made at outer corner of the eye (second lash made) (page 36, images 3–6). Pull yarn needle through top of Head and cut yarn. Begin stuffing the Head. Continue stuffing the Head firmly every few rounds.

Rnd 23: 1 sc in each st around.

Rnd 24: *1 sc in next 3 sts, inv dec in next 2 sts; repeat from * around. (24 sc)

Rnd 25: *1 sc in next 2 sts, inv dec in next 2 sts; repeat from * around. (18 sc)

Rnd 26: *1 sc in next st, inv dec in next 2 sts; repeat from * around. (12 sc)

Rnds 27–28: 1 sc in each st around.

Fasten off, leaving a long tail.

Put the Head aside for now. Continue with Arms.

Arm (make 2)

Rnd 1: With skin-tone yarn, make a magic ring, 6 sc into ring, pull ring closed. (6 sc)

Rnd 2: 2 sc in each st around. (12 sc)

Start stuffing the Arms around Rnd 5 and continue to stuff every few rounds, being careful not to overstuff.

Rnds 3–28: 1 sc in each st around.

Fasten off, leaving a long tail.

Put the Arms aside until needed for the Body.

First Leg

Rnd 1: With skin-tone yarn, starting with a magic ring, 7 sc into ring, pull ring closed. (7 sc)

Rnd 2: 2 sc in each st around. (14 sc)

Rnds 3–30: 1 sc in each st around.

Start stuffing the legs around Rnd 5 and continue to stuff every few rounds, being careful not to overstuff.

Fasten off. Weave in ends, but leave a st marker in the last st.

Second Leg

Work the Second Leg the same as the First Leg through Rnd 29.

Rnd 30: 1 sc in next 13 sts, change to underwear color yarn, 1 sc in next st. (14 sc) (images 1–2)

Fasten off the skin-tone yarn, and weave in the ends. Continue with Underwear color yarn to complete the Underwear.

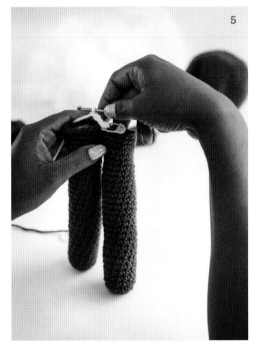

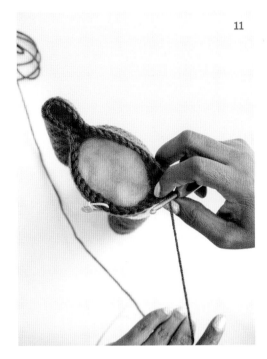

11

12

Underwear & Body

You will now join the Legs together and then work the Underwear and upper Body. Note that after joining the Legs, there will be a small hole that will be sewn up later.

Rnd 1: Starting with Second Leg, ch 3; working on the First Leg, 1 sc in the 1st st after the marked st and next 13 sts, remove marker from First Leg, ch 3; working on the Second Leg, 1 sc in 1st st after the marked st and next 13 sts. (28 sc, 6 chs) (page 39, images 3–6)

The marker from the Second Leg can now be used to keep track of rounds.

Rnds 2–7: 1 sc in each st around. (34 sc)

Stuff every few rnds.

Rnd 8: 1 sc in next 11 sts, inv dec in next 2 sts, 1 sc in next 14 sts, inv dec in next 2 sts, 1 sc in next 5 sts, change to skin-tone yarn. (32 sc)

Fasten off the Underwear color yarn, and weave in the ends.

Rnds 9–18: 1 sc in each st around. (opposite, image 7)

You will join in the Arms on Rnd 19. Be sure the Arms are as close to the same position on each side as possible. If you notice that one Arm is more forward or farther back than the other, it is okay to join in the Arm at a stitch forward or back from what is listed in the pattern. You will still be able to follow along with the pattern even if you must join in on a different stitch.

Rnd 19: 1 sc in next 13 sts, 1 sc in 1st st on the first Arm and next 11 sts around the first Arm. 1 sc in next 15 sts of the Body, 1 sc in 1st st of the second Arm and next 11 sts of the second Arm, 1 sc in remaining 4 sts of the Body. (56 sc) (pages 40–41, images 8–12)

Rnd 20: 1 sc in each st around.

Rnd 21: *1 sc in next 12 sts, inv dec in next 2 sts; repeat from * around. (52 sc)

Rnd 22: *1 sc in next 2 sts, inv dec in next 2 sts; repeat from * around. (39 sc)

Rnd 23: *1 sc in next st, inv dec in next 2 sts; repeat from * around. (26 sc)

Rnd 24: 1 sc in each st around.

Rnd 25: [1 sc in next 2 sts, inv dec in next 2 sts] 6 times, 1 sc in next 2 sts. (20 sc)

Rnd 26: [Inv dec in next 2 sts, 1 sc in next st] 6 times, inv dec in next 2 sts. (13 sc)

Rnd 27: 1 sc in next 11 sts, inv dec in next 2 sts. (12 sc)

Rnds 28–29: 1 sc in each st around.

Fasten off, leaving a long tail.

On the Body, you will notice small holes from the Arm join; you can close those holes with the long tail you left on the arms using a tapestry needle. You will also still have the hole from the Leg join. Do not close this hole just yet, as you will need it later.

(right and opposite, images 13–18)

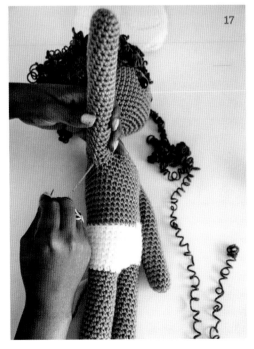

1

3

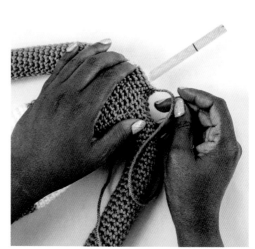

2

4

5

6

Assembly

The Head attaches to the Body using a wooden dowel. Cut the dowel down to approximately 9 inches (23 cm) long. Depending on the yarn used and tension, the dowel may need to be slightly shorter or longer. The most important thing is that one end of the dowel touches the top of the Head, and the other end of the dowel fits at the Leg join where there is a small hole. To make sure you have the correct measurement, insert the dowel through the neck of the Body and out through the hole at the Leg join. Mark off with a pen or pencil on the dowel where it sits directly at the Leg join.

Add additional polyester fiberfill around the neck and wooden dowel. Using a yarn needle and the long tail from the neck of the Body, sew the neck closed around the dowel. Fit the Head over the neck of the Body, being sure that the wooden dowel is touching the top of the Head. Make sure the Head is facing forward, and using a yarn needle and the long tail from the Head, sew the Head to the body using a running stitch. (opposite, images 1–3) Trim the dowel so that it sits right at the Leg join. Once the dowel is cut down, sew up the hole at the Leg join. The Head should be securely attached to the Body. (images 4–6)

1

2

Finishing Details

You have your base doll and now you can add some finishing details that will allow you to put your own creative spin on the design. An important aspect to remember in making a My Pretty Brown Doll design is that there is more to making a brown doll than just using brown yarn. The hairstyle you choose, how you dress the doll, and other cultural aspects you add are what will add the magic to your design. Below are some finishing details that I include to add more personality and cultural representation to my designs.

Nose

Embroider the Nose using skin-tone yarn and a yarn needle. Center the nose between the two eyes, lining it up with the bottom of the eyes. Insert the yarn needle and bring the needle back up three to four stitches over. Insert the needle back through the same stitch it went in before. Repeat this process three to four times or until the Nose is the desired thickness. Weave the tail of the yarn through the Head and then cut. (images 1–2)

Mouth

The original My Pretty Brown Doll design does not include a mouth. However, if you would like for your doll design to have a mouth/lips, you can add an embroidered mouth using a small amount of white yarn for teeth and then embroidering an outline around the teeth using skin-tone yarn. The other option is to use a precut felt mouth/lips. I have found precut felt doll lips on Etsy and Amazon; you can secure the felt mouth/lips to the doll's face using E6000 glue or fabric glue of your choice.

Ear (make 2)

The Ears are one of the last things I add to the design mainly because I am able to use the hairstyle and doll arms as a guide for where to sew on the Ears. To make the Ears, you will use a size US G/6 (4 mm) crochet hook and worsted-weight (4) yarn in the same color you used for the head.

Row 1: Start with magic ring, 6 hdc in ring, pull ring closed. Turn. (6 hdc)

Row 2: Sl st across. Fasten off, leaving a long tail.

Use the tail to sew the ears onto the Head. Line the Ears up with the shoulders. The top part of the Ears should be on the same round as the Eyes.
(images 3–4)

Hairstyles

One of the things I love about creating doll designs is not just celebrating the pretty in every shade of brown but also exploring hairstyles that can be created with yarn and that are inspired by all the different styles of natural hair. The hairstyle you choose may be one of the most important aspects of your design. Below you will find instructions for some of the most popular hairstyles I've created.

~~~~~~~~~~~~~~~~~~~~

NOTE: *All the hairstyles call for a Wig Cap or base hair covering. This works great for short hairstyles and can look complete on its own!*

Wig Cap

Using the worsted-weight (4) yarn, follow the instructions for the doll Head from Rnds 1–18 (see page 34). Try the Wig Cap on the doll. It should fit snugly and sit slightly back. If you find that the Wig Cap seems a little short or too long, you can add an additional round or take a round out. Once the Wig Cap is fitted properly, fasten off and leave a long tail. Using the long tail, sew the Wig Cap to the head using a running stitch.

Afro Puffs

The Afro Puffs hairstyle is almost like a rite of passage in the African American culture. No matter how small or big the puffs, the moment your hair can be pulled into two puffs, it is almost like your Black Girl Magic has been activated!

What You Need

Approximately 40 yd (36 m) chunky-weight (5) yarn in desired color. Yarn used is Yarn Bee Fleece Lite in the color Black.

Yarn needle

3⅜-inch (8.5 cm) pom-pom maker

4½-inch (11.5 cm) pom-pom maker

Stitch marker

Scissors

Afro Puff (make 2)

There are a lot of ways to make pom-pom Afro Puffs. A pom-pom maker makes the process much faster. I can get cute and even puffs quickly. For texture and fullness, use a chunky-weight (5) yarn to make the puffs. However, you can also create awesome puffs with worsted-weight (4) yarn. Make two Afro Puffs approximately 3⅜ inches (8.5 cm). Sew the puffs onto the Wig Cap using the same yarn as the Wig Cap.

Use your yarn needle and the worsted-weight (4) yarn to sew the puffs into place on the Wig Cap. Use the photo at left as a guide.

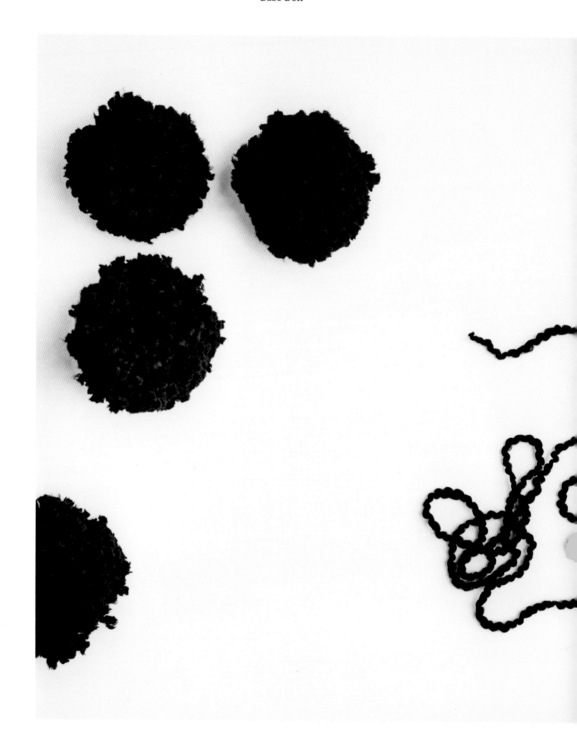

Variation: One Afro Puff

To create the one Afro Puff hairstyle, make the Wig Cap as stated above. Make one pom-pom puff approximately 4½ inches (11.5 cm) big. Sew the puff to the top of the Wig Cap using the same yarn used for the Wig Cap.

Variation: Low Side Afro Puff

This hairstyle is great for the Paris Outfit (page 128) because it allows the beret to fit properly. Follow the instructions for the Two Afro Puffs hairstyle, but only make one puff. Sew the puff to the Wig Cap either at the lower left or lower right side.

Ponytails

Ponytails are another popular hairstyle, but what makes them unique are all the hair bobbles and barrettes you can add.

What You Need

Approximately 110 yd (100 m) chunky-weight (5) yarn in desired color. Yarn used is Yarn Bee Fleece Lite in the color Black.

Size US G/6 (4 mm) crochet hook

Hair bobbles or barrettes

Rubber bands

Scissors

Using chunky-weight (5) yarn, cut strands of yarn approximately 15 inches (38 cm) long.

Secure the strands to the Wig Cap using a lark's head knot as follows: Fold a strand in half. Use the crochet hook to pull the folded loop through the Wig Cap. Bring the tails of yarn through the loop and pull to tighten and secure.

As you attach the yarn strands into the Wig Cap, be mindful of where you want your ponytails to be placed. Start around the edges of the Wig Cap and then fill in the middle. Once you have the strands in place, use the rubber bands to section off and create your Ponytails. Use your bobbles to wrap around the rubber bands, and then section your strands into equal parts. Twist and add a barrette at the end to hold the twist in place. Trim any excess yarn on ends.

To create the middle part, use a strand of skin-tone yarn that measures from the front edge of the Wig Cap to the back edge. Using a yarn needle, thread one end of the skin-tone yarn through the middle front edge of the Wig Cap, lay the yarn down the middle of the Wig Cap, and secure the other end at the back edge. Cut off any excess yarn.

Curls for Days

The Curls for Days hairstyle is one of the more time-consuming, but the end result is always worth it, which is why it is one of my favorites.

What You Need

Approximately 95 yd (87 m) worsted-weight (4) yarn in the same color as the Wig Cap. Yarn used is Lion Brand Skein Tones in the color Adobe. Note: Acrylic yarn works best for this technique.

Size US G/6 (4 mm) crochet hook

Wooden dowels (approximately 12)

Hair dryer

Scissors

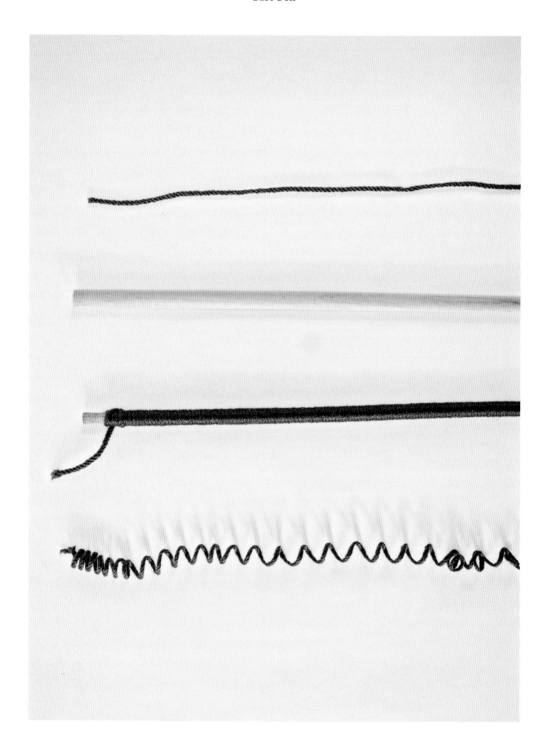

To make the Curls, wrap the yarn around each wooden dowel tightly, creating a slip knot when you get to the end of the dowel to secure the yarn in place. Once you have each dowel wrapped, cut the yarn from the ball. Submerge the wrapped wooden dowels in very hot water for approximately 20 minutes. Use a towel to squeeze out any excess water, then use a hair dryer to dry the yarn while it is wrapped around the dowels. Be sure the yarn is completely dry before removing from dowels. I normally leave my dowels out overnight to ensure they are completely dry. Once the yarn is dry, remove from the dowels and cut the curly strands to the length you would like for your doll design. The pictured doll has strands that were approximately 3 inches (7.5 cm) long with a light stretch in the curls.

Attach the strands to the Wig Cap using a lark's head knot to get the look you would like to achieve as follows: Fold each strand in half. Use the crochet hook to pull the loop through the Wig Cap. Bring the ends of the strand through the loop, and pull to tighten and secure. These curls can be used for ponytails, Mohawks, and even Afros.

Outfits

Basic Wardrobe

Now that you have completed the body and hairstyle of the My Pretty Brown Doll design, you can focus on making an outfit. You have several outfits to choose from, including the classic Mia outfit, a ballerina outfit, a soccer uniform, a mermaid design, and more. You can choose bright bold colors, more subtle colors, or even mix and match pieces to give your design a brand-new look. Note that some designs will include nonremovable clothes that may require you to make modifications to the base design. If this is the case, it will be noted at the beginning of the outfit pattern.

Here are some of the most basic wardrobe pieces for your doll. These can be created in any color, and you can try a number of designs from stripes to polka dots to adding fringe—whatever your skill set allows for!

What You Need
Size US E/4 (3.5 mm) crochet hook
Size US F/5 (3.75 mm) crochet hook
Size US G/6 (4 mm) crochet hook
Stitch marker
Yarn needle
Small amount polyester fiberfill
See individual patterns for yarn recommendations

Pattern Notes
Adjust hook size based on what was used to achieve the gauge/measurements for the base doll. Work in continuous rounds. Use a stitch marker in the last stitch of the round to keep track of rounds.

At the end of a piece worked in the round, join with a slip stitch in the first stitch before you fasten off.

Long-Sleeve Top

Yarn

Approximately 100 yd (91 m) worsted-weight (4) yarn in color of your choice. Yarn used is I Love This Cotton in the color Bright Green.

Sleeve (make 2)

Using E/4 (3.5 mm) hook, ch 17; join with a sl st in 1st ch, being careful not to twist.

Rnd 1: 1 sc in each ch around. (17 sc)

Rnd 2: 1 hdc in BLO in each st around.

Rnds 3–15: 1 hdc in each st around.

At end of last rnd, fasten off, leaving a long tail.

Body

Using E/4 (3.5 mm) hook, ch 32, join with a sl st in 1st ch, being careful not to twist.

Rnd 1: 1 sc in each st around. (32 sc)

Rnds 2–7: 1 hdc in each st around.

Note: You will now join the Sleeves to the Body on Rnd 8, using a similar method to the one that was used to join the Arms on the Body of the doll.

Rnd 8: 1 hdc in next 11 sts, 1 hdc in 1st st and next 16 sts of the first Sleeve, 1 hdc in next 14 sts of the Body, 1 hdc in the 1st st and next 16 sts of the second Sleeve, 1 hdc in the remaining 7 sts of the Body. (66 hdc)

Rnd 9: 1 sc in each st around.

Rnd 10: *1 sc in next 3 sts, inv dec in next 2 sts; repeat from * 13 times, 1 sc in last st. (53 sc)

Rnd 11: *1 sc in next 2 sts, inv dec in next 2 sts; repeat from * 13 times, 1 sc in last st. (40 sc)

Rnd 12: 1 sc in each st around.

Rnd 13: *1 sc in next st, inv dec in next 2 sts; repeat from * 13 times, 1 sc in last st. (27 sc)

Fasten off. Weave in ends. Use the yarn tails from the Sleeves to close the small hole from the Sleeves join.

Pants

Yarn

Approximately 100 yd (91 m) worsted-weight (4) yarn in color of your choice. Yarn used is I Love This Yarn in the color Black.

First Leg

Using F/5 (3.75 mm) hook, ch 18; join with a sl st in 1st ch, being careful not to twist.

Rnd 1: 1 sc in each ch around. (18 sc)

Rnds 2–26: 1 sc in each st around.

Fasten off.

Second Leg

Work the Second Leg the same as the First, but do not fasten off.

Rnd 27: Ch 3, 1 sc in 1st st and next 17 sts on the First Leg, ch 3, 1 sc in 1st st and next 17 sts on the Second Leg. (36 sc, 6 chs)

Rnd 28: 1 sc in each st around. (42 sc)

Rnds 29–35: 1 sc in each st around.

Rnd 36: *1 sc in next 5 sts, inv dec in next 2 sts, repeat from * around. (36 sc)

Rnd 37: 1 sc in each st around.

Rnd 38: *1 sc in next 4 sts, inv dec in next 2 sts, repeat from * around. (30 sc)

Rnd 39: 1 sc in each st around.

Rnd 40: Sl st in each st around.

Fasten off. Weave in ends.

Shoe (make 2)

Yarn

Approximately 20 yd (18 m) worsted-weight (4) yarn for soles and approximately 20 yd (18 m) worsted-weight (4) yarn for top of shoes. Yarn used for sole is I Love This Yarn in the color Black. Yarn used for top of Shoe is I Love This Yarn in the color Red.

For the Shoes, you can decide if you want the sole and top of the Shoes to be all one color or if you want to use one color for the sole and another color for the top.

Rnd 1: Using F/5 (3.75 mm) hook and desired color, ch 8, 1 sc in 2nd ch from the hook, 1 sc in next 5 chs, 7 hdc in last ch, rotate to work on the opposite side of the ch, 1 sc in next 6 sts. (19 sts)

Rnd 2: 2 sc in next st, 1 sc in next 5 sts, 2 sc in next 7 sts, 1 sc in next 6 sts. (27 sc)

Rnd 3: 1 sc in each st around.

Note: If desired, change to top-of-shoe color at the end of Rnd 3.

Rnd 4: 1 sc in BLO in each st around.

Rnd 5: Inv dec in next 2 sts, 1 sc in next 7 sts, [inv dec in next 2 sts] 5 times, 1 sc in next 8 sts. (21 sc)

Rnd 6: 1 sc in next 6 sts, [inv dec in next 2 sts] 4 times, 1 sc in next 5 sts, inv dec in next 2 sts. (16 sc)

Rnd 7: Sl st in each st around. Fasten off. Weave in ends.

Add a small amount of polyester fiberfill in the front of the Shoe for shape. The Shoes should fit your doll's feet snugly.

Cross-Body Bag

Rnd 1: Using F/5 (3.75 mm) hook, starting with a magic ring, 8 sc into ring, pull ring closed. (8 sc)

Rnd 2: 2 sc in each st around. (16 sc)

Rnd 3: *1 sc in next st, 2 sc in next st; repeat from * around. (24 sc)

Rnd 4: *1 sc in next 3 sts, 2 sc in next st; repeat from * around. (30 sc)

Rnds 5–12: 1 sc in each sc around.

At the end of Rnd 12, ch 24 or number needed for bag strap to hang comfortably on doll when crossed over her shoulders. Sl st to opposite side of bag. Fasten off. Weave in ends.

Yarn

Approximately 60 yd (55 m) worsted-weight (4) yarn in color of your choice. Yarn used is Caron Simply Soft in the color Black.

Infinity Scarf

Headscarf

One of my favorite hair accessories to add to the doll design is a fabric Headscarf. I normally choose an ankara-print fabric. Cut the fabric down to fit the doll's head, approximately 38 inches (96.5 cm) to 42 inches (106.5 cm) long and about 8 inches (20.5 cm) wide. Fold the two long edges in so the fabric strip is approximately 4½ inches (11.5 cm) wide. Depending on the doll's hairstyle, I will normally wrap the Headscarf to cover the back of the head, with the ends up above the head, then twist the two ends together and wind it down around itself, creating a topknot. Then just tuck in the ends. That will secure the Headscarf but still allow it to be removable. This works really well for the One Puff hairstyle with the puff coming out the top, but it will also work if you decide to cover all of the hair.

Again, the goal is for you to be able to add your own creative spin to the design. Think outside the box and know that the only limitation in bringing your design to life is your own mind.

Yarn

Approximately 80 yd (73 m) worsted-weight (4) yarn in color of your choice. Yarn used is I Love This Yarn in the color Red.

Using G/6 (4 mm) hook, ch 64; join with a sl st in 1st ch, being careful not to twist.

Rnd 1: Ch 2 (does not count as a stitch here or throughout), dc in each ch around, join with sl st to 1st dc. (64 dc)

Rnds 2–5: Ch 2, 1 dc in each st around, join with sl st to 1st dc.

Fasten off. Weave in ends.

Scarf should wrap around doll's neck at least two times comfortably.

School Uniform

The inspiration for this outfit is all the first-day-of-school pictures I've seen on social media, particularly my Instagram feed. The awesome thing about the school uniform pattern is that you can create it to match your school colors.

~~~~~~~~~~~~~~~~~~~~~~~~~~~~~~~~~

What You Need
Size US E/4 (3.5 mm) crochet hook
Size US F/5 (3.75 mm) crochet hook
Stitch marker
Yarn needle
Velcro strip or Velcro dots to close back of dress
½-inch (12 mm) button for backpack
Small amount polyester fiberfill
Hot glue gun and glue stick, or sewing needle and thread
See individual patterns for yarn recommendations

Pattern Notes
Adjust hook size based on what was used to achieve the gauge/measurements for the base doll.

Work in continuous rounds. Use a stitch marker in the last stitch of the round to keep track of rounds.

At the end of a piece worked in the round, join with a slip stitch in the first stitch before you fasten off.

Chain 1 at the end of a row does not count as a stitch.

Dress

Yarn

Approximately 100 yd (91 m) worsted-weight (4) yarn in color of your choice. Yarn used is I Love This Yarn in the color Navy.

Row 1: Using F/5 (3.75 mm) hook, ch 35, 1 sc in 2nd ch from hook and each ch across, ch 1, turn. (34 sc)

Rows 2–9: 1 sc in each st across, ch 1, turn.

Rnd 10: 1 sc in BLO, sl st in 1st sc of row.

Note: You will now be working in the round.

Rnd 11: 2 sc in each st around. (68 sc)

Rnd 12: *1 sc in next sts, 2 sc in next st; repeat from * around. (102 sc)

Rnds 13–26: 1 sc in each st around.

Fasten off. Weave in ends.

Strap (make 2)

Row 1: Using F/5 (3.75 mm) hook, ch 14, 1 sc in 2nd ch from hook and each ch across, ch 1, turn. (13 sc)

Row 2: 1 sc in each st across, ch 1, turn.

Row 3: 1 sc in each st across.

Fasten off. Weave in ends.

Neckline

Join yarn in 1st st at the top left back of the Dress.

Rnd 1: Working in other side of foundation ch, 1 sc in next 11 sts, 1 hdc in next 2 sts, sl st in next 9 sts, 1 hdc in next 2 sts, 1 sc in next 10 sts.

Fasten off. Weave in ends.

Sew Straps on at the hdc sts on the front of the Dress and approximately 3 sts over on the back of the Dress, leaving enough room to add Velcro strips or dots to close the back of the dress.

To close up the back of the dress, cut Velcro strips approximately 2½ to 3 inches (6 to 7.5 cm) long. Hot-glue the rough side of the Velcro strip to the left side of the opening of the dress, then hot-glue the smooth side to the inside of the right side of the dress. You can also use two or three sets of ⅝-inch (1.5 cm) Velcro dots. Hot-glue the rough side of a Velcro dot to the left side of the dress and the smooth side to the inside of the right side of the dress. If you prefer not to use hot glue, you can use a sewing needle and thread the same color as the dress to hand-sew the edges of the Velcro to the dress.

Top

Yarn

Approximately 75 yd (69 m) worsted-weight (4) yarn in color of your choice. Yarn used is I Love This Yarn in the color White.

Using F/5 (3.75 mm) hook, ch 28; join with a sl st in 1st ch, being careful not to twist.

Rnd 1: 1 sc in ch around. (28 sc)

Rnds 2–11: 1 sc in each st around.

Rnd 12: 1 sc in next 7 sts, ch 12, 1 sc in next 14 sts, ch 12, 1 sc in next 7 sts. (28 sc, 24 chs)

Rnd 13: 1 sc in each sc and ch around. (52 sc)

Rnd 14: 1 sc in each st around. (52 sc)

Rnd 15: [1 sc in next 2 sts, inv dec in next 2 sts] 12 times, 1 sc in next 4 sts. (40 sc)

Rnd 16: Inv dec in next 2 sts, [1 sc in next st, inv dec in next 2 sts] 12 times, inv dec in next 2 sts. (26 sc)

Rnd 17: 1 sc in each st around.

Fasten off. Weave in ends.

To put the Top on the doll, pull it up over the doll's legs, as it will not fit over the doll's head.

Backpack

Yarn

Approximately 60 yd (55 m) worsted-weight (4) yarn in color of your choice. Yarn used is I Love This Yarn in the color yellow.

Rnd 1: Using E/4 (3.5 mm) hook, ch 13, 1 sc in 2nd ch from the hook, 1 sc in next 10 chs, 3 sc in next ch, rotate to work on opposite side of ch, 2 sc in next ch, 1 sc in next 9 sts, 3 sc in last ch. (28 sc)

Rnd 2: 2 sc in next st, 1 sc in next 11 sts, 2 sc in next st, 1 sc in next st, 2 sc in next st, 1 sc in next 11 sts, 2 sc in next st, 1 sc in last st. (32 sc)

Rnd 3: 1 sc in next st, 2 sc in next st, 1 sc in next 11 sts, 2 sc in next st, 1 sc in next 3 sts, 2 sc in next st, 1 sc in next 11 sts, 2 sc in next st, 1 sc in next 2 sts. (36 sc)

Rnd 4: 1 sc in BLO in each st around.

Rnds 5–17: 1 sc in each st around.

Rnd 18: *1 sc in next 7 sts, inv dec in next 2 sts; repeat from * around. (32 sc)

Fasten off. Weave in ends.

Strap (make 2)

Using E/4 (3.5 mm) hook, ch 60. Fasten off. Weave in ends.

Lay Backpack flat to find center. Space straps evenly from center, along each side. Weave each Strap through the bottom of the Backpack. Knot the ends inside the Backpack to secure.

Flap

Note: There are 16 sts on the back side of the Backpack. The flap is worked in the 9 sts approximately in the middle.

With the front side of the Backpack facing you, join the yarn in the 1st of the 9 center sts.

Row 1: Working in FLO, sc in same st as the join and next 3 sts, ch 5, skip 1 st, 1 sc in next 4 sts, ch 1, turn. (8 sc, 5 chs)

Row 2: 1 sc in 1st sc, 2 sc in next sc, 1 sc in next 2 sc, 1 sc in skipped sc, 1 sc in next 2 sc, 2 sc in next sc, 1 sc in next sc, ch 1, turn. (11 sc)

Row 3: 1 sc in each st across, ch 1, turn.

Row 4: 1 sc in next 2 sts, 2 sc in next st, 1 sc in next 5 sts, 2 sc in next st, 1 sc in next 2 sts, ch 1, turn. (13 sc)

Row 5: 1 sc in each st across, ch 1, turn.

Row 6: 1 sc in next 3 sts, 2 sc in next st, 1 sc in next 5 sts, 2 sc in next st, 1 sc in next 3 sts, ch 1, turn. (15 sc)

Row 7: 1 sc in next 7 sts, ch 3, skip 1 st, 1 sc in next 7 sts, ch 1, turn. (14 sc, 3 chs)

Row 8: 1 sc in next 7 sts, sl st in the ch-3 space, 1 sc in next 7 sts.

Fasten off. Weave in ends.

Sew button between Rnds 13 and 14, matching up with the button loop that was created.

Shoe (make 2)

Yarn
Approximately 40 yd (37 m) worsted-weight (4) yarn in color of your choice. Yarn used is I Love This Yarn in Navy Blue for the top of the Shoes and I Love This Yarn in the color White for the soles.

You can make the same Shoes from Mia's Basic Wardrobe pattern (page 70), or if you would like to make a Mary Jane–inspired shoe, follow the Basic Wardrobe Shoe pattern through Rnd 6.

Rnd 7: Sl st in next 6 sts, ch 5, skip 5 sts, sl st in next 5 sts.

Fasten off. Weave in ends.

Add a small amount of polyester fiberfill in the front of the Shoe for shape. The Shoes should fit your doll's feet snugly.

Collegiate Sweatshirt

This college-inspired sweatshirt is a great alternative to the School Uniform (page 74). The collegiate sweatshirt outfit can be created by using the pattern below, along with the Pants (page 69) from the Basic Wardrobe or the Tulle Tutu (page 99) from the Ballerina.

~~~~~~~~~~~~~~~~

What You Need

Approximately 110 yd (100 m) worsted-weight (4) yarn in color of your choice. Yarn used is Yarn Bee Soft Secret in the color Navy.

Size US E/4 (3.5 mm) crochet hook

Size US F/5 (3.75 mm) crochet hook

Stitch marker

Yarn needle

Iron-on vinyl or letter stickers and fabric glue (optional)

Pattern Notes

Adjust hook size based on what was used to achieve the gauge/measurements for the base doll.

Work in continuous rounds. Use a stitch marker in the last stitch of the round to keep track of rounds.

At the end of a piece worked in the round, join with a slip stitch in the first stitch before you fasten off.

Sleeve (make 2)

Using F/5 (3.75 mm) hook, ch 15; join with a sl st in 1st ch, being careful not to twist.

Rnd 1: 1 sc in each ch around. (15 sc)

Rnd 2: 1 sc in each st around.

Rnd 3: Working in BLO, [1 hdc in next 3 sts, 2 hdc in next st] 3 times, 1 hdc in last 3 sts. (18 hdc)

Change to E/4 (3.5 mm) hook.

Rnds 4–20: 1 hdc in each st around. (18 hdc)

Rnd 21: *1 hdc in next st, hdc dec in next 2 sts; repeat from * around. (12 hdc)

Fasten off, leaving a long tail.

Body

Using F/5 (3.75 mm) hook, ch 30; join with a sl st in 1st ch, being careful not to twist.

Rnd 1: 1 sc in each ch around. (30 sc)

Rnd 2: 1 sc in each st around. (30 sc)

Rnd 3: Working in BLO, [1 hdc in next 4 sts, 2 hdc in next st] 6 times. (36 hdc)

Change to E/4 (3.5 mm) hook.

Rnds 4–8: 1 hdc in each st around.

Rnd 9: *1 hdc in next 4 sts, hdc dec in next 2 sts; repeat from * around. (30 hdc)

Note: You will join the Sleeves to the Body on Rnd 10, using a similar method to the one that was used to join the Arms on the Body of the doll.

Rnd 10: 1 hdc in next 11 sts, 1 hdc in the 1st st and each st of first Sleeve around, 1 hdc in next 15 sts of the Body, 1 hdc in 1st st and each st of second Sleeve around, 1 hdc in the remaining 4 sts of the Body. (54 hdc)

Rnd 11: 1 hdc in each st around.

Rnd 12: 1 hdc in next 11 sts, hdc dec in next 2 sts, 1 hdc in next 8 sts, hdc dec in next 2 sts, 1 hdc in next 15 sts, hdc dec in next 2 sts, 1 hdc in next 8 sts, hdc dec in next 2 sts, 1 hdc in next 4 sts. (50 hdc)

Rnd 13: [1 hdc in next 2 sts, hdc dec in next 2 sts] 12 times, 1 hdc in last 2 sts. (38 sts)

Rnd 14: [1 hdc in next st, hdc dec in next 2 sts] 12 times, 1 hdc in last 2 sts. (26 sts)

Rnd 15: 1 sc in each st around.

Rnd 16: Sl st in each st around. Fasten off. Weave in ends.

To personalize your sweater, add a college university name using iron-on vinyl with a mini iron or with small letter stickers adhered with fabric glue.

The Scientist

Next up is one of my favorite designs! Normally when we think about scientists, we don't think about girls, and we think even less about girls of color in those roles. But we need to—imagine what all kids can grow up to achieve if only they're encouraged to follow their dreams. This outfit was made to inspire little Brown girls everywhere that they really can be anything they set their minds to, scientist included.

Your doll can wear the Long-Sleeve Top (page 68) or the School Uniform Top (page 79). Pair with the Pants (page 69) and the Shoes (page 70), in any color you want, from the Basic Wardrobe.

~~~~~~

What You Need
Size US E/4 (3.5 mm) crochet hook
Size US F/5 (3.75 mm) crochet hook
Stitch marker
⅝-inch (1.5 cm) white button
Yarn needle
See individual patterns for yarn recommendations

Pattern Notes
The Lab Coat is made with a back panel, two front panels (one with button loop), and sleeves.

Work in continuous rounds. Use a stitch marker in the last stitch of the round to keep track of rounds.

At the end of a piece worked in the round, join with a slip stitch in the first stitch before you fasten off.

Chain 1 at the end of a row does not count as a stitch.

Lab Coat

Yarn

Approximately 120 yd (110 m) worsted-weight (4) yarn in color of your choice. Yarn used is I Love This Yarn in the color White.

Back

Row 1: Using F/5 (3.75 mm) hook, ch 23, 1 sc in 2nd ch from hook, 1 sc in each ch across, ch 1, turn. (22 sc)

Rows 2–32: 1 sc in each st across, ch 1, turn.

Row 33: 1 sc in next 9 sts, inv dec in next 2 sts, 1 sc in next 9 sts, inv dec in next 2 sts, ch 1, turn. (20 sc)

Row 34: 1 sc in next 8 sts, inv dec in next 2 sts, 1 sc in next 8 sts, inv dec in next 2 sts, ch 1, turn. (18 sc)

Row 35: 1 sc in next 7 sts, inv dec in next 2 sts, 1 sc in next 7 sts, inv dec in next 2 sts, ch 1, turn. (16 sc)

Row 36: 1 sc in next 6 sts, inv dec in next 2 sts, 1 sc in next 6 sts, inv dec in next 2 sts, ch 1, turn. (14 sc)

Row 37: 1 sc in each st across, ch 1, turn.

Row 38: 1 sc in each st across.

Fasten off. Weave in ends.

Left Front Panel

Row 1: Using F/5 (3.75 mm) hook, ch 14, 1 sc in 2nd ch from the hook, 1 sc in each ch across, ch 1, turn. (13 sc)

Rows 2–10: 1 sc in each st across, ch 1, turn.

Row 11: 1 sc in each st, ch 4, sl st in last st worked into (button loop made), ch 1, turn. (13 sc, 4 chs)

Row 12: Skip ch-4 space, 1 sc in each sc across, ch 1, turn.

Rows 13–32: 1 sc in each st across, ch 1, turn.

Row 33: Inv dec in next 2 sts, 1 sc in next 11 sts, ch 1, turn. (12 sc)

Row 34: 1 sc in next 10 sts, inv dec in next 2 sts, ch 1, turn. (11 sc)

Row 35: Inv dec in next 2 sts, 1 sc in next 9 sts, ch 1, turn. (10 sc)

Row 36: 1 sc in next 8 sts, inv dec in next 2 sts, ch 1, turn. (9 sc)

Row 37: 1 sc in each st across, ch 1, turn.

Row 38: 1 sc in each st across.

Fasten off. Weave in ends.

Right Front Panel

Rows 1–32: Make as for Left Front Panel.

Row 33: 1 sc in next 11 sts, inv dec in next 2 sts, ch 1, turn. (12 sc)

Row 34: Inv dec in next 2 sts, 1 sc in next 10 sts, ch 1, turn. (11 sc)

Row 35: 1 sc in next 9 sts, inv dec in next 2 sts, ch 1, turn. (10 sc)

Row 36: Inv dec in next 2 sts, 1 sc in next 8 sts, ch 1, turn. (9 sc)

Row 37: 1 sc in each st across, ch 1, turn.

Row 38: 1 sc in each st across.

Fasten off. Weave in ends.

Sleeve (make 2)

Using F/5 (3.75 mm) hook, ch 18; join with a sl st in 1st ch, being careful not to twist.

Rnd 1: 1 sc in each ch around. (18 sc)

Rnds 2–18: 1 sc in each around.

Fasten off, leaving a long tail.

Pocket (make 2)

Row 1: Using F/5 (3.75 mm) hook, ch 9, 1 sc in 2nd ch from hook, 1 sc in each ch across, ch 1, turn. (8 sc)

Rows 2–5: 1 sc in each st across, ch 1, turn.

Row 6: 1 sc in each st across.

Fasten off. Weave in ends.

Lab Coat Finishing

Assemble the Lab Coat inside out so that the seams will be on the inside of the coat. Line up the Back and two Front Panels with the right sides facing each other. Using your yarn needle and matching yarn, sew the sides up to the decrease rows, fasten off, and weave in ends. Sew the shoulder seams starting at the arm edge and sewing together three stitches across, fasten off, and weave in ends. To attach the Sleeves, lay the Sleeves inside the coat, lining the top of the Sleeve as closely as possible with the armhole. Sew the Sleeve to the armhole as evenly as possible. Fasten off and weave in ends. Turn the coat right side out. Sew on Pockets approximately two rows below button loop. Line your button up with the button loop on the opposite panel. Sew on button.

Collar

Using F/5 (3.75 mm) hook and matching yarn, join yarn at the right corner of the neck opening. 2 dc in the same st as the join, 1 sc in each st around neck opening, ending with 2 dc in last st on left front, fasten off, and weave in ends.

The lab coat is complete and your doll is ready to crush it at the district science fair.

Safety Glasses

Yarn

Approximately 50 yd (46 m) worsted-weight (4) yarn in color of your choice. Yarn used is I Love This Yarn in the color White for the eye glasses and I Love This Yarn in the color Black for the straps.

Eye Glass (make 2)

Rnd 1: Using E/4 (3.5 mm) hook and white yarn, ch 24, join to beginning ch with sl st being careful not to twist, 1 sc in each ch around. (24 sc)

Rnds 2–3: 1 sc in each st around.

Rnd 4: 1 sc in BLO in each st around.

Rnds 5–7: 1 sc in each st around.

Fold Rnds 5–7 inward. This will move your working yarn to the inside of the Eye Glass.

Working in BLO of current rnd and through beginning ch, sl st around.

Fasten off. Weave in ends.

Glasses Strap

Rnd 1: Using E/4 (3.5 mm) hook and desired color, ch 43, 1 dc in 5th ch from hook, 1 dc in next 3 chs, 1 hdc in next 5 chs, 1 sc in next 5 chs, sl st in next 10 chs, 1 sc in next 5 chs, 1 hdc in next 5 chs, 1 dc in next 5 chs.

Fasten off. Weave in ends.

Sew the ends of the Glasses Strap to the sides of the Eye Glasses. Sew the two Eye Glasses together in the middle. The Safety Glasses should slide onto the head easily but fit snugly.

This completes the outfit of your design.

Tip: Why stop at scientist? Doctors wear lab coats, too! Pair doll scrubs with the lab coat to inspire a budding doctor you know.

The Ballerina

The next outfit is another favorite: the classic ballerina. This outfit does require you to modify the base pattern, as the top for the ballerina outfit is nonremovable.

~~~~~~

What You Need

Skin Tone: Approximately 130 yd (119 m) worsted-weight (4) yarn in color of your choice. Yarn used is I Love This Yarn in the color Toasted Almond.

Leotard: Approximately 55 yd (50 m) worsted-weight (4) yarn in color of your choice. Yarn used is I Love This Yarn in the color Jelly Bean.

See individual patterns for yarn recommendations

Size US F/5 (3.75 mm) crochet hook

Or size needed to obtain gauge

Size US G/6 (4 mm) crochet hook

Stitch marker

Yarn needle

Polyester fiberfill

¼-inch- (6 mm) wide ribbon for ballet slippers (optional)

3-inch- (7.5 cm) wide tulle, approximately 8 yd (7.3 m), or as much as needed to achieve desired skirt fullness

⅜-inch- (1 cm) wide ribbon for skirt, approximately 10 inches/ 25 cm (should be snug around the doll, with enough for a bow in the back)

5 × 8-inch (13 × 20 cm) piece cardboard (a DVD case will work well)

Small amount black yarn or embroidery thread for eyelashes and eyebrows (optional)

⅜-inch (1 cm) diameter × 12-inch- (30.5 cm) long dowel

Handsaw or strong scissors to cut the dowel

Fabric scissors

Finished Measurements

Approximately 15½ inches (39.5 cm) tall

Gauge

5 rounds = 2½ inches (6 cm) in sc using US F/5 (3.75 mm) hook

Pattern Notes

Work in continuous rounds. Use a stitch marker in the last stitch of the round to keep track of rounds.

At the end of a piece worked in the round, join with a slip stitch in the first stitch before you fasten off.

To get recital-ready, we will need to make a few changes to the base design.

Head, Arms, Legs, Eyes, Nose, and Mouth

Follow the base design for the Head, Arms, Eyes, Nose, and Mouth (pages 34–49). For the Legs, follow the base design (page 38), but instead of changing to an underwear color, change to the color of yarn for the leotard.

Body

Using the leotard-color yarn only, follow Base Doll Design directions for Rnds 1–23 (see pages 41–42) of the Underwear & Body. At end of Rnd 23, change to skin-tone yarn.

Rnd 24: 1 sc in BLO in each st around. (26 sc)

Rnd 25: [1 sc in next 2 sts, inv dec in next 2 sts] 6 times, 1 sc in next 2 sts. (20 sc)

Rnd 26: [Inv dec in next 2 sts, 1 sc in next st] 6 times, inv dec in next 2 sts. (13 sc)

Rnd 27: 1 sc in next 11 sts, inv dec in next 2 sts. (12 sc)

Rnds 28–29: 1 sc in each st around.

Fasten off, leaving a long tail. Follow Assembly instructions (page 47) for Base Doll Design

Tulle Tutu

First, cut the ribbon to the desired length; the ribbon should wrap around the waist and be long enough to be tied into a nice bow. The ribbon should be snug, but not too tight.

Wrap the tulle around a piece of cardboard to cut strips approximately 8 inches (20 cm) long. (This allows you to cut several strips at once.) Once the tulle is wrapped, cut across one side of the cardboard. Fold a strip of tulle in half to form a loop. Pull the ends of the tulle over the ribbon and through the loop, creating a lark's head knot around the ribbon. Continue attaching strips of tulle until skirt is at the desired fullness. I add tulle until I can't move it along the ribbon. Trim the tulle ends so that they are even, and then you have the perfect tutu for your doll.

Ballet Slipper (make 2)

Rnd 1: Using G/6 (4 mm) hook, ch 8, 1 sc in 2nd ch from hook, 1 sc in next 5 chs, 3 sc in last ch, rotate to work on the opposite side of the ch, 1 sc in next 5 chs, 2 sc in last ch. (16 sc)

Rnd 2: 1 sc in next 6 sts, 2 sc in next 3 sts, 1 sc in next 7 sts. (19 sc)

Rnd 3: 1 sc in BLO in each st around.

Rnd 4: 1 sc in next 6 sts, 1 hdc in next 6 sts, 1 sc in next 7 sts.

Rnd 5: Sl st in next 6 sts, [inv dec in next 2 sts] 3 times, sl st in next 7 sts. (16 sts)

Rnd 6: Ch 2, skip 1 st, sl st in next st.

Fasten off. Weave in ends. To finish your Ballet Slippers, make a ch of 60 sts and weave through the loop created in round 6, criss-cross the ch up the doll leg two times, and then tie into a bow on the back of the doll's leg.

Optional: Instead of a ch, take a ribbon and use the same method as you would with the ch to finish off the Ballet Slipper.

Now your ballerina is ready to dance!

Yarn

Approximately 40 yd (37 m) worsted-weight (4) yarn in color of your choice. Yarn used is I Love This Yarn in the color Jelly Bean.

Fairy Wings

Want to turn your ballerina into a mystical fairy?
You can do so by adding wings!

~~~~~~~~~~~~~~~~~~~~~~~~~~~~~~~~~~~~

What You Need

Approximately 20 yd (18 m)
   worsted-weight (4) yarn in
   desired color. Yarn used is
   I Love This Yarn Metallic in
   Blush Sparkle.
Size US E/4 (3.5 mm) crochet hook
Stitch marker
Yarn needle
Scissors

Pattern Notes

Work in continuous rounds. Use a
stitch marker in the last stitch of
the round to keep track of rounds.

At the end of a piece worked in the
round, join with a slip stitch in the
first stitch before you fasten off.

Wing Top (make 2)

Rnd 1: Ch 13, 1 sc in 2nd ch from hook and next 3 sts, 1 hdc in next 4 sts, 1 dc in next 3 sts, (2 dc, 1 tr, 2 dc) in last st, rotate to work on opposite side of the ch, 1 dc in next 3 sts, 1 hdc in next 4 sts, 1 sc in next 4 sts. (27 sts)

Rnd 2: 2 sc in next st, 1 sc in next 12 sts, 2 sc in next st, picot st, 2 sc in next st, 1 sc in next 12 sts. (30 st)

Fasten off. Weave in ends.

Wing Bottom (make 2)

Rnd 1: Ch 8, 1 sc in 2nd ch from hook and next st, 1 hdc in next 2 sts, 1 dc in next 2 sts, (2 dc, 1 tr, 2 dc) in last st, rotate to work on opposite side of ch, 1 dc in next 2 sts, 1 hdc in next 2 sts, 1 sc in next 2 sts. (17 sts)

Rnd 2: 2 sc in next st, 1 sc in next 6 sts, 2 sc in next 3 sts, 1 sc in next 7 sts. (21 sc)

Fasten off. Weave in ends.

Assembly

Sew the Wing Bottoms to the bottom parts of the Wing Tops. The Wing Bottoms should be pointing downward and the Wing Tops pointing outward. Sew the two wings together at the center. If you would like your wings to be non-removable, sew them to the back of your ballerina. If you would like the wings to be removable, join yarn in the back center of the wings, ch 45, and sl st close to where you joined the yarn on the back. Repeat this step to form a second loop. Slide the arms of the ballerina doll into the chain loops.

Softball Uniform

Ready to go from recital to softball field? The softball uniform is one of the more detailed outfits, but it is lots of fun to make. Again, you can make it your own by choosing your favorite school or team colors.

TIP: *No need to be softball specific. This pattern easily passes for a baseball uniform!*

What You Need
Size US F/5 (3.75 mm) crochet hook
Stitch marker
Yarn needle
Five ⅝-inch (15 mm) buttons
Small amount polyester fiberfill
See individual patterns for yarn recommendations

Pattern Notes
Work in continuous rounds. Use a stitch marker in the last stitch of the round to keep track of rounds.

At the end of a piece worked in the round, join with a slip stitch in the first stitch before you fasten off.

Chain 1 at the end of a row does not count as a stitch.

Shirt

Yarn

Approximately 100 yd (91 m) worsted-weight (4) yarn in desired color. Yarn used is I Love This Yarn in the color Mixed Berry.

Row 1: Ch 41, 1 sc in 2nd ch from hook and each ch across, ch 1, turn. (40 sc)

Row 2: 1 sc in each st across, ch 5 (for button loop), turn.

Rows 3–5: 1 sc in each st across, ch 1, turn.

Rows 6–13: Repeat Rows 2–5 twice.

Row 14: Repeat Row 2.

Row 15: Repeat Row 3.

Row 16: 1 sc in next 11 sts, ch 12, 1 sc in next 18 sts, ch 12, 1 sc in next 11 sts, ch 1, turn. (40 sc, 24 chs)

Row 17: 1 sc in each st across, ch 1, turn. (64 sc)

Row 18: Repeat Row 2.

Row 19: *1 sc in next 2 sts, inv dec in next 2 sts; repeat from * across, ch 1, turn. (48 sc)

Row 20: *1 sc in next st, inv dec in next 2 sts; repeat from * across, ch 1, turn. (32 sc)

Row 21: [1 sc in next st, inv dec in next 2 sts] 10 times, 1 sc in next 2 sts. (22 sc)

Fasten off. Weave in ends.

Sleeve (make 2)

Join yarn in any ch of sleeve opening.

Rnd 1: Sc in the same ch as the join and each ch around. (12 sc)

Rnd 2: [1 sc in next 3 sts, 2 sc in next] 3 times. (15 sc)

Rnds 3–16: Sc in each st around.

Fasten off. Weave in ends.

Pants

Yarn

Approximately 100 yd (91 m) worsted-weight (4) yarn in desired color. Yarn used is I Love This Yarn in the color Yellow with the accent stripe in Mixed Berry.

Leg (make 2)

Rnd 1: Ch 22; join with a sl st to beginning ch, being careful not to twist, 1 sc in each st around. (22 sc)

Rnds 2–25: Sc in each st around.

Fasten off first Leg. Do not fasten off second Leg.

Upper

Rnd 26: Ch 3, 1 sc in 1st st and next 21 sts on first Leg, ch 3, sc in 1st st after the ch 3 on second Leg and next 21 sts of second Leg. (44 sc, 6 chs)

Rnds 27–34: 1 sc in each st around. (50 sc)

Rnd 35: *1 sc in next 3 sts, inv dec in next 2 sts; repeat from * around. (40 sc)

Rnd 36: 1 sc in each st around.

Rnd 37: [1 sc in next 4 sts, inv dec in next 2 sts] 6 times, 1 sc in next 4 sts. (34 sc)

Rnd 38: 1 sc in each st around.

Fasten off. Weave in ends.

Using shirt-color yarn, make 2 chains of 25. Sew the chains to each side of the pants.

Sock (make 2)

Yarn

Worsted-weight (4) yarn in desired color. Yarn used is I Love This Yarn in the color Mixed Berry.

Rnd 1: Starting with a magic ring, 7 sc in ring, pull ring closed. (7 sc)

Rnd 2: 2 sc in each st around. (14 sc)

Rnds 3–10: 1 sc in each st around.

Fasten off. Weave in ends.

Shoe (make 2)

Note: Shoes can be one color or two.

Yarn

Worsted-weight (4) yarn in desired color. Yarn used is I Love This Yarn in the color Black with a small amount of I Love This Yarn in the color White for the laces.

Sole

Rnd 1: Using desired color, ch 8, 1 sc in 2nd ch from hook, 1 sc in next 5 chs, 7 hdc in the last ch, rotate to work on the opposite side of ch, 1 sc in next 6 chs. (19 sts)

Rnd 2: 2 sc in next st, 1 sc in next 5 sts, 2 sc in next 7 sts, 1 sc in next 6 sts. (27 sc)

Rnd 3: 1 sc in each st around.

Note: If desired, for a two-tone shoe like in the Parisian Look (see page 129), change to side-of-shoe color at the end of Rnd 3.

Rnd 4: 1 hdc in next 10 sts, 1 dc in next 7 sts, 1 hdc in next 10 sts.

Fasten off. Weave in ends.

Tongue

With the front of the Shoe facing, join yarn in the 1st dc st of previous rnd.

Row 1: 1 sc in BLO in same st as join and next 6 sts, ch 1, turn. (7 sc)

Row 2: Inv dec in next 2 sts, 1 sc in next 3 sts, inv dec in next 2 sts, ch 1, turn. (5 sc)

Rows 3–5: 1 sc in each st across, ch 1, turn.

Row 6: Inv dec in next 2 sts, 1 sc in next st, inv dec in next 2 sts. (3 sc)

Fasten off. Weave in ends.

Sides

With the front of the Shoe facing, join yarn in hdc closest to front.

Row 1: 1 sc in the same hdc as join and each hdc around, ch 1, turn. (20 sc)

Row 2: *1 sc in next st, inv dec in next 2 sts; repeat from * 5 times, 1 sc in next 2 sts. (14 sc)

Fasten off. Weave in all ends.

Add a small amount of polyester fiber-fill inside the front of the Shoe for shape. The Shoes should fit your doll's feet snugly.

Cut a length of yarn and use a yarn needle to weave through sides of Shoes as shoelaces. Tie the laces into a nice bow.

Finishing Touches

Using a yarn needle and the yellow yarn used for the Pants, or yarn to match your buttons, sew the buttons on the Shirt to match up with the buttonholes previously created.

Tuck Pants Leg in the Socks or fold under toward the inside of the pant legs to create a baggy look and show off Socks.

Soccer Uniform

Because girls play soccer too! This is another fun sports uniform that you can make your own just by changing the yarn colors to match your favorite team.

~~~~~~~~~~~~~~~~

What You Need

Size US F/5 (3.75 mm) crochet hook
Stitch marker
Yarn needle
Small amount polyester fiberfill
See individual patterns for yarn recommendations

Pattern Notes

Work in continuous rounds. Use a stitch marker in the last stitch of the round to keep track of rounds.

At the end of a piece worked in the round, join with a slip stitch in the first stitch before you fasten off.

Chain 1 at the end of a row does not count as a stitch.

Shorts

Yarn

Approximately 60 yd worsted-weight (4) yarn in desired color. Yarn used is I Love This Yarn in the color Navy Blue (base) and I Love This Yarn Metallic in the color Blush Sparkle (accent).

Rnd 1: Ch 30, join with a sl st, being careful not to twist. 1 sc in each st around. (30 sc)

Rnds 2–5: 1 sc in each st around. (30 sc)

Rnd 6: *1 sc in the next 5 sts, 2 sc in the next st; repeat from * around. (35 sc)

Rnd 7: 1 sc in each st around.

Rnd 8: *1 sc in the next 6 sts, 2 sc in the next st; repeat from * around. (40 sc)

Rnd 9: 1 sc in each st around.

Rnd 10: *1 sc in the next 7 sts, 2 sc in the next st; repeat from * around. (45 sc)

Rnd 11: 1 sc in each st around.

Rnd 12: *1 sc in the next 8 sts, 2 sc in the next st; repeat from * around. (50 sc)

Rnd 13: 1 sc in the next 24 sts, skip next 25 sts, 1 sc in last st. (This will create the leg holes for the shorts.)

Rnd 14: You will be working around one leg hole, 1 sc in each st around. (25 sc)

Rnd 15: 1 sc in each st around. (25 sc)

Fasten off. Weave in ends.

Join in yarn on second leg hole.

Rnds 16–18: 1 sc in each st around. (25 sc)

Fasten off. Weave in ends

Stripe (make 4)

With accent color yarn, ch 17, leaving a long tail. Using the long tail and a yarn needle, sew two of the chains along each side of the shorts.

Shirt

Yarn

Approximately 100 yd (91 m) worsted-weight (4) yarn in desired color. Yarn used is I Love This Yarn Metallic in the color Blush Sparkle (accent) and I Love This Yarn in the color White (base).

Sleeve (make 2)

Rnd 1: With base color, ch 18, join with a sl st, being careful not to twist, 1 sc in each ch. Change to accent color at the end of this round. (18 sc)

Rnds 2–7: 1 sc in each st around.

Rnd 8: *1 sc in next st, sc dec; repeat from * around. (12 sc)

Fasten off. Weave in ends.

Body

Rnd 1: With base color, ch 42, join with sl st, being careful not to twist, 1 sc in each st around. (42 sc)

Rnds 2–5: 1 sc in each st around.

Rnd 6: *1 sc in next st, sc dec; repeat from * around. (36 sc)

Rnds 7–10: 1 sc in each st around.

Rnd 11: *1 sc in the next st, sc dec; repeat from * around. (30 sc)

Rnds 12–15: 1 sc in each st around. Change to accent color at end of this round.

Note: You will now join the Sleeves to the Body on Rnd 16, using a similar method to the one that was used to join the Arms on the Body of the doll.

Rnd 16: 1 sc in the next 8 sts of the body of the shirt, 1 sc in the 12 sts around one of the sleeves, 1 sc in the next 14 sts of the body of the shirt, 1 sc in 12 sts around the sleeve, 1 sc in next 8 sts of the body of the shirt. (54 sc)

Rnd 17: 1 sc in each st around.

Rnd 18: [1 sc in the next 6 sts, sc dec] 6 times, 1 sc in the next 6 sts. (48 sc)

Rnd 19: *1 sc in the next 2 sts, sc dec; repeat from * around. (36 sc)

Rnd 20: *1 sc in the next 2 sts, sc dec; repeat from * around. (27 sc)

Rnd 21: 1 sl st in each st around.

Fasten off. Weave in ends.

You may have small holes where you connected the Sleeves to the Body of the Shirt. You can close up those holes by using your accent color yarn and yarn needle.

Sock & Shoe (make 2 each)

Make the Shoes and Socks following the patterns for the Softball Uniform (pages 110–111), using Blush Sparkle for the Socks and Navy Blue for the Shoes, with a small amount of White for the laces.

The Mermaid

The mermaid design is another deviation from the original base pattern. You will make the head and arms the same as the base pattern, and then follow these pattern instructions to complete the design. The mermaid design can wear any of the hairstyles from pages 52–61. The design pictured is wearing a swim cap, which is the Wig Cap from page 52. This design also uses purple yarn for eye shadow and store-bought eyelashes for added fun.

~~~~~~~~~~~~~~~~~~~~~~~~~~~~~~~~~~~~~~~

What You Need

Skin Tone: Approximately 120 yd (110 m) worsted-weight (4) yarn in color of your choice. Yarn used is I Love This Cotton in the color Brown.

Fins and Tail: Approximately 120 yd (110 m) worsted-weight (4) yarn in color of your choice. I used Impeccable Yarn in the color Skylight.

See individual patterns for yarn recommendations

Size US F/5 (3.75 mm) crochet hook

Or size needed to obtain gauge

Stitch marker

Yarn needle

Small amount black yarn or embroidery thread for eyelashes and eyebrows (optional)

⅜-inch (1 cm) diameter × 12-inch- (30.5 cm) long dowel

Handsaw or strong scissors to cut dowel

Flat jewels and craft glue (optional)

Finished Measurements

Approximately 18 inches (45.5 cm) tall

Gauge

5 rounds = 2½ inches (6 cm) in sc using US F/5 (3.75 mm) hook

Pattern Notes

Work in continuous rounds. Use a stitch marker in the last stitch of the round to keep track of rounds.

At the end of a piece worked in the round, join with a slip stitch in the first stitch before you fasten off.

Head and Arms

Follow the base design on pages 34–38.

First Fin

Rnd 1: Starting with a magic ring, 4 sc into ring, pull ring closed. (4 sc)

Rnd 2: 1 sc in each st around.

Rnd 3: 2 sc in each st around. (8 sc)

Rnd 4: *2 sc in next st, 1 sc in next 3 sts; repeat from * around. (10 sc)

Rnd 5: *2 sc in next st, 1 sc in next 4 sts; repeat from * around. (12 sc)

Rnd 6: *1 sc in next 5 sts, 2 sc in next st; repeat from * around. (14 sc)

Rnd 7: *2 sc in next st, 1 sc in next 6 sts; repeat from * around. (16 sc)

Rnd 8: *1 sc in next 7 sts, 2 sc in next st; repeat from * around. (18 sc)

Rnds 9–12: 1 sc in each st around.

Rnd 13: *Inv dec in next 2 sts, 1 sc in next 7 sts; repeat from * around. (16 sc)

Rnd 14: *Inv dec in next 2 sts, 1 sc in next 6 sts; repeat from * around. (14 sc)

Rnd 15: *Inv dec in next 2 sts, 1 sc in next 5 sts; repeat from * around. (12 sc)

Rnd 16: *Inv dec in next 2 sts, 1 sc in next 4 sts; repeat from * around. (10 sc)

Rnd 17: *Inv dec in next 2 sts, 1 sc in next 3 sts; repeat from * around. (8 sc)

Rnd 18: *Inv dec in next 2 sts, 1 sc in next 2 sts; repeat from * around. (6 sc)

Fasten off. Weave in ends.

Second Fin

Work the same as First Fin, but do not fasten off. Continue with the Tail.

Tail

Note: The Tail starts by joining the two fins together.

Rnd 1: 1 sc in 1st st on First Fin and in next 5 sts on the same fin, 1 sc in each st of Second Fin. (12 sc)

Rnd 2: *Inv dec in next 2 sts, 1 sc in next 2 sts; repeat from * around. (9 sc)

Rnd 3: Inv dec in next 2 sts, 1 sc in next 3 sts, 2 sc in next st, 1 sc in next 3 sts.

Rnd 4: 1 sc in next 4 sts, 2 sc in next st, 1 sc in next 4 sts. (10 sc)

Rnd 5: 1 sc in next 4 sts, 2 sc in next st, 1 sc in next 5 sts. (11 sc)

Rnd 6: 1 sc in next 4 sts, 2 sc in next st, 1 sc in next st, 2 sc in next st, 1 sc in next 4 sts. (13 sc)

Rnd 7: 1 sc in each st around.

Rnd 8: 1 sc in next 6 sts, 2 sc in next st, 1 sc in next 6 sts. (14 sc)

Rnd 9: 1 sc in next 6 sts, 2 sc in next 2 sts, 1 sc in next 6 sts. (16 sc)

Rnd 10: 1 sc in each st around.

Rnd 11: 1 sc in next 7 sts, 2 sc in next st, 1 sc in next 8 sts. (17 sc)

Rnd 12: 1 sc in next 6 sts, 2 sc in next st, 1 sc in next 2 sts, 2 sc in next st, 1 sc in next 7 sts. (19 sc)

Rnd 13: 1 sc in each st around.

Begin stuffing and continue stuffing every few rounds.

Rnd 14: 1 sc in next 9 sts, 2 sc in next st, 1 sc in next 9 sts. (20 sc)

Rnd 15: 1 sc in next 9 sts, 2 sc in next st, 1 sc in next 10 sts. (21 sc)

Rnd 16: 1 sc in next 20 sts, 2 sc in next st. (22 sc)

Rnd 17: 1 sc in each st around.

Rnd 18: 1 sc in next 9 sts, 2 sc in next st, 1 sc in next 9 sts, 2 sc in next st, 1 sc in next 2 sts. (24 sc)

Rnd 19: 1 sc in next 20 sts, 2 sc in next st, 1 sc in next 2 sts, 2 sc in next st. (26 sc)

Rnd 20: 1 sc in next 10 sts, 2 sc in next st, 1 sc in next 15 sts. (27 sc)

Rnd 21: 1 sc in next 24 sts, 2 sc in next st, 1 sc in next 2 sts. (28 sc)

Rnd 22: 1 sc in next 22 sts, 2 sc in next st, 1 sc in next 4 sts, 2 sc in next st. (30 sc)

Rnd 23: 1 sc in next 10 sts, 2 sc in next st, 1 sc in next 19 sts. (31 sc)

Rnd 24: 1 sc in next 26 sts, 2 sc in next st, 1 sc in next 4 sts. (32 sc)

Rnd 25: 1 sc in next 24 sts, 2 sc in next st, 1 sc in next 4 sts, 2 sc in next st, 1 sc in next 2 sts. (34 sc)

Rnd 26: 1 sc in next 10 sts, 2 sc in next st, 1 sc in next 23 sts. (35 sc)

Rnd 27: 1 sc in next 28 sts, 2 sc in next st, 1 sc in next 6 sts. (36 sc)

Rnd 28: 1 sc in next 26 sts, 2 sc in next st, 1 sc in next 4 sts, 2 sc in next st, 1 sc in next 4 sts. (38 sc)

Rnd 29: 1 sc in next 26 sts, 2 sc in next st, 1 sc in next 5 sts, 2 sc in next st, 1 sc in next 5 sts. (40 sc)

Rnds 30–31: 1 sc in each st around.

Rnd 32: 1 sc in next 32 sts, [inv dec in next 2 sts] 4 times. (36 sc)

Change to skin-tone yarn at the end of Rnd 32.

Body

Rnd 33: Working in the BLO, 1 sc in next 11 sts, inv dec in next 2 sts, 1 sc in next 18 sts, inv dec in next 2 sts, 1 sc in next 3 sts. (34 sc)

Rnd 34: 1 sc in each st around.

Rnd 35: 1 sc in next 8 sts, [inv dec in next 2 sts] 2 times, 1 sc in next 16 sts, [inv dec in next 2 sts] 2 times, 1 sc in next 2 sts. (30 sc)

Rnds 36–43: 1 sc in each st around.

Note: You will join the Arms on Rnd 44. Be sure the Arms are as close to the same position on each side as possible. If you notice that one Arm is more forward or farther back than the other, it is okay to join the Arm at a stitch or two before or after what is listed in the pattern. You will still be able to follow along with the pattern even if you must join in on a different stitch.

Rnd 44: 1 sc in next 10 sts, 1 sc in 1st st and next 11 sts of the first Arm, 1 sc in next 15 sts of Body, 1 sc in 1st st and next 11 sts of second Arm, 1 sc in remaining 5 sts of Body. (54 sc)

Rnd 45: 1 sc in each st around.

Rnd 46: 1 sc in next 9 sts, inv dec in next 2 sts, 1 sc in next 9 sts, inv dec in next 2 sts, 1 sc in next 14 sts, inv dec in next 2 sts, 1 sc in next 10 sts, inv dec in next 2 sts, 1 sc in next 4 sts. (50 sc)

Rnd 47: [1 sc in next 2 sts, inv dec next 2 sts] 12 times, 1 sc in next 2 sts. (38 sc)

Rnd 48: [Inv dec in next 2 sts, 1 sc in next 2 sts] 9 times, 1 sc in next 2 sts. (29 sc)

Rnd 49: [1 sc in next st, inv dec in next 2 sts] 9 times, 1 sc in next 2 sts. (20 sc)

Rnd 50: Inv dec in next 2 sts, 1 sc in next 8 sts, inv dec in next 2 sts, 1 sc in next 8 sts. (18 sc)

Rnd 51: 1 sc in each st around.

Rnd 52: *1 sc in next st, inv dec in next 2 sts; repeat from * around. (12 sc)

Rnds 53–54: 1 sc in each st around.

Fasten off, leaving a long tail.

On the Body, you will notice small holes from the Arm join; you can close those holes with the long tail you left on the Arms. Follow Assembly instructions (page 47) for the base doll. You will connect the Head of the mermaid in the same way as in Base Doll Design. The dowel should touch from the top of the head to where the fins are connected.

If desired, embellish the tail with flat jewels that can be applied with craft glue or fabric glue.

Star Top

Yarn

Approximately 30 yd (27 m) worsted-weight (4) yarn in color of your choice. I used Impeccable Yarn in the color Violet.

Rnd 1: Starting with a magic ring, [1 sc, 1 dc, ch 2, sl st in 2nd ch from hook, 1 dc] 5 times in ring, pull ring closed. Fasten off the first star and weave in ends.

Make a second star the same, but do not fasten off. Ch 3, sl st to the center back of first star, ch 24, sl st back on second star to connect. Fasten off and weave in ends. The star top will slide up over the tail onto the body; it should fit snug around the chest area.

If desired, make a third star for a hair ornament; use a yarn needle and the same color yarn used to make the star and sew onto the Wig Cap at desired location. For the Wig Cap, I used Impeccable Yarn in the color Petunia.

Parisian Look

This outfit is one of my favorites. It is inspired by a trip I took to Paris for my birthday. I even had the pleasure of taking a Mia doll design on the trip with me. My favorite part of this design is definitely her low side puff and her beret.

~~~~~~~~~~~~~~~~~~~~~~~~~~

What You Need

Size US E/4 (3.5 mm) crochet hook
Size US F/5 (3.75 mm) crochet hook
Size US G/6 (4 mm) crochet hook
Stitch marker
Yarn needle
Scissors
Small amount of polyester fiberfill
Sewing needle and thread
Two $^{13}/_{16}$-inch (20 mm) buttons
See individual patterns for yarn recommendations

Pattern Notes

Adjust hook size based on what was used to achieve the gauge/measurements for the base doll.

Work in continuous rounds unless otherwise stated. Use a stitch marker in the last stitch of the round to keep track of rounds.

At the end of a piece worked in the round, join with a slip stitch in the first stitch before you fasten off.

Chain 1 at the beginning of a round does not count as a stitch.

The coat is worked from the top down.

Dress

Yarn

Top and Skirt: Approximately 100 yd (92 m) worsted-weight (4) yarn in color of your choice. Yarn used is Caron Simply Soft in the color Black.

Top: Approximately 15 yd (14 m) worsted-weight (4) yarn in color of your choice. Yarn used is Caron Simply Soft in the color White.

Top

Rnd 1: Using US F/5 (3.75 mm) hook, with black yarn, ch 29, 1 sc in 2nd ch from hook and each ch across; join with a slip st to 1st sc, being careful not to twist. (28 sc)

Rnd 2: 1 sc in each st around.

Note: Change to white yarn at the end of Rnd 2, and continue to alternate between black and white yarn for each round.

Rnd 3: 1 sc in BLO in each st around.

Rnds 4–9: 1 sc in each st around.

Rnd 10: 1 sc in next 7 sts, ch 12, 1 sc in next 14 sts, ch 12, 1 sc in next 7 sts. (28 sc, 24 chs)

Rnds 11–12: 1 sc in each st around. (52 sc)

Rnd 13: [1 sc in next 2 sts, inv dec in next 2 sts] 12 times, 1 sc in next 4 sts. (40 sc)

Rnd 14: Inv dec in next 2 sts, [1 sc in next st, inv dec in next 2 sts] 12 times, inv dec in next 2 sts. (26 sc)

Rnd 15: 1 sc in each st around.

Fasten off. Weave in ends.

Peacoat

Skirt

Note: Do not alternate between black and white yarn for this portion of the dress. Work in one color only. The sample is shown in black.

Hold Top of Dress so that the bottom edge is facing up. Using US F/5 (3.75 mm) hook, join yarn in any unworked front loop from Rnd 2 of the Top.

Rnd 1: 1 sc in each FLO around. (28 sc)

Rnd 2: 2 dc in each st around. (56 dc)

Rnd 3: *1 dc in next st, 2 dc in next st; repeat from * around. (84 dc)

Rnd 4: *1 dc in next 2 sts, 2 dc in next st; repeat from * around. (112 dc)

Rnd 5: *1 dc in next 3 sts, 2 dc in next st; repeat from * around. (140 dc)

Rnds 6–8: 1 dc in each st around.

Rnd 9: 1 sc in each st around.

Fasten off. Weave in ends.

Yarn

Approximately 200 yd (183 m) worsted-weight (4) yarn in color of your choice. Yarn used is I Love This Yarn Metallic in the color Red.

Body

Row 1: Using F/5 (3.75 mm) hook, ch 25, 1 sc in the 2nd ch from hook and each st across, ch 1, turn. (24 sts)

Row 2: 1 sc in each st across, ch 1, turn.

Row 3: [1 sc in next 3 sts, 2 sc in next st] 3 times, [2 sc in next st, 1 sc in next 3 sts] 3 times, ch 1, turn. (30 sc)

Row 4: 1 sc in each st across, ch 1, turn.

Row 5: [1 sc in next 4 sts, 2 sc in next st] 3 times, [2 sc in next st, 1 sc in next 4 sts] 3 times, ch 1, turn. (36 sc)

Row 6: 1 sc in each st across, ch 1, turn.

Row 7: [1 sc in next 2 sts, 2 sc in next st] 6 times, [2 sc in next st, 1 sc in next 2 sts] 6 times, ch 1, turn. (48 sc)

Rows 8–9: 1 sc in each st across, ch 1, turn.

Row 10: 1 sc in next 8 sts, ch 7, skip 10 sts (armhole made), 1 sc in next 12 sts, ch 7, skip 10 sts (armhole made), 1 sc in next 8 sts, ch 1, turn. (28 sc, 14 chs)

Rows 11–13: 1 sc in each st across, ch 1, turn. (42 sc)

Row 14: 1 sc in BLO in each st across, ch 1, turn.

Change to smaller hook.

Row 15: 2 dc in each st across, ch 1, turn. (84 dc)

Rows 16–21: 1 dc in each st across, ch 1, turn.

Row 22: 1 dc in each st across.

Fasten off. Weave in ends.

Add Sleeves

Using F/5 (3.75 mm) hook, join yarn on Row 10 at the armhole.

Rnd 1: 1 sc in each ch and skipped sc around armhole. (17 sc)

Rnds 2–32: 1 sc in each st around.

Fasten off. Weave in ends. The sleeves should be long enough that you can fold them up approximately 3 rounds to create a cuffed sleeve.

Collar

Using F/5 (3.75 mm) hook, join yarn at corner in 1st st at neck opening.

Row 1: Evenly crochet 24 sc around top of coat, ch 1, turn. (24 sc)

Row 2: 2 sc in 1st st, 1 sc in next 22 sts, 2 sc in last st. (26 sc)

Fasten off. Weave in ends.

Button Loops

Using G/4 (3.5 mm) hook, join yarn in edge of Row 13 on the right edge of coat. Sl st in 2 row edges, ch 4, sl st in next 3 row edges, ch 4, sl st in next 6 row edges. Fasten off. Weave in ends.

Using the sewing needle and thread, sew in the buttons on the coat's left front side, across from each button loop.

Beret

Yarn

Approximately 110 yd (100 m) worsted-weight (4) yarn in color of your choice. Yarn used is I Love This Yarn in the color Red.

Rnd 1: Using US F/5 (3.75 mm) hook, with red yarn, starting with a magic ring, 6 sc into ring, pull ring closed. (6 sc)

Rnd 2: Ch 1, 2 sc in each st around, sl st in 1st sc. (12 sc)

Rnd 3: Ch 1, *1 sc in next st, 2 sc in next st; repeat from * around, sl st in 1st sc. (18 sc)

Rnd 4: Ch 1, *1 sc in next 2 sts, 2 sc in next st; repeat from * around, sl st in 1st sc. (24 sc)

Rnd 5: Ch 1, *1 sc in next 3 sts, 2 sc in next st; repeat from * around, sl st in 1st sc. (30 sc)

Rnd 6: Ch 1, *1 sc in next 4 sts, 2 sc in next st; repeat from * around, sl st in 1st sc. (36 sc)

Rnd 7: Ch 1, *1 sc in next 5 sts, 2 sc in next st; repeat from * around, sl st in 1st sc. (42 sc)

Rnd 8: Ch 1, *1 sc in next 6 sts, 2 sc in next st; repeat from * around, sl st in 1st sc. (48 sc)

Rnd 9: Ch 1, *1 sc in next 7 sts, 2 sc in next st; repeat from * around, sl st in 1st sc. (54 sc)

Rnd 10: Ch 1, *1 sc in next 8 sts, 2 sc in next st; repeat from * around, sl st in 1st sc. (60 sc)

Rnd 11: Ch 1, *1 sc in next 9 sts, 2 sc in next st; repeat from * around, sl st in 1st sc. (66 sc)

Rnd 12: Ch 1, *1 sc in next 10 sts, 2 sc in next st; repeat from * around, sl st in 1st sc. (72 sc)

Rnd 13: Ch 1, *1 sc in next 11 sts, 2 sc in next st; repeat from * around, sl st in 1st sc. (78 sc)

Rnd 14: Ch 1, *1 sc in next 12 sts, 2 sc in next st; repeat from * around, sl st in 1st sc. (84 sc)

Rnd 15: Ch 1, *1 sc in next 13 sts, 2 sc in next st; repeat from * around, sl st in 1st sc. (90 sc)

Rnd 16: Ch 1, *1 sc in next 14 sts, 2 sc in next st; repeat from * around, sl st in 1st sc. (96 sc)

Rnds 17–18: Ch 1, 1 sc in each st around, sl st in 1st sc.

Rnd 19: Ch 1, *1 sc in next 4 sts, inv dec in next 2 sts; repeat from * around, sl st in 1st sc. (80 sc)

Rnd 20: Ch 1, *1 sc in next 3 sts, inv dec in next 2 sts; repeat from * around, sl st in 1st sc. (64 sc)

Rnd 21: Ch 1, *1 sc in next 2 sts, inv dec in next 2 sts; repeat from * around, sl st in 1st sc. (48 sc)

Rnds 22–23: Ch 1, 1 sc in each st around, sl st in 1st sc.

Fasten off. Weave in ends.

Shoes

Make the Shoes (page 70) following the pattern from Basic Wardrobe, using Black for the soles and Red for the sides, or your desired color(s).

Resources

Brown Skin-Tone Yarns

Red Heart Soft in Chocolate
Red Heart Soft in Toast
Red Heart Soft in Wheat
I Love This Cotton in Brown
I Love This Cotton in Antique Gold
I Love This Cotton in Taupe
I Love This Yarn in Toasted Almond
I Love This Yarn in Coffee
I Love This Yarn in Brown
Lion Brand Skein Tones in Adobe
Lion Brand Skein Tones in Mahogany
Lion Brand Skein Tones in Ebony
Lion Brand Skein Tones in Cedarwood
Lion Brand Skein Tones in Honey
Lion Brand Skein Tones in Cocoa

Yarns Used for Clothes

I Love This Cotton in Bright Green
I Love This Yarn in Jelly Bean
I Love This Yarn in Fire Red
I Love This Yarn in Navy Blue
I Love This Yarn in Black
I Love This Yarn in White
I Love This Yarn Metallic in Red
I Love This Yarn Metallic in Blush Sparkle
Yarn Bee Soft Secret in Navy
Caron Simply Soft in Black
Caron Simply Soft in White
Impeccable Yarn in Yellow
Impeccable Yarn in Skylight
Impeccable Yarn in Violet
Impeccable Yarn in Petunia

Yarns Used for Hair

Caron Simply Soft in Black
Yarn Bee Fleece Lite in Black
Lion Brand Skein Tones in Adobe

Hooks

Clover Soft Touch

Fiberfill

Fairfield Poly-fil, 100 percent polyester

Acknowledgments

This book is dedicated to my mom, Georgia Hill, who was a constant reminder that no matter how many times I fall, I have the strength to get up again. I hope that you are looking down from heaven and are proud of the work I am doing.

A special thank-you to Meredith Clark, my editor at Abrams, for believing I was the right person to bring this book to life. Your encouragement and patience with me from the very beginning are one of the main reasons this book is a book!

To my friend Aniqua Wilkerson, the first person I called to share the news and the person who stayed up with me until I hit the submit button on the due date. I will never be able to truly express what our friendship means to me, but you already know: "It ain't me, but it is me!"

To my Instagram and Facebook followers, thank you for allowing me to not only share my work but to share *me*. Your enthusiasm and excitement for my work is what allowed me to keep going on the days I wanted to quit. Every like, share, and DM to encourage me to keep going was and still is much appreciated.

To my family, Lonnie, Jolon, and baby "J," thanks for making sure I did not starve, and that I got out of the house sometimes. To my aunt Barbara, whose good-morning texts reminded me that I had something to be grateful for every single day, thank you for not missing a day in over two years. To my dad, Garson, thanks for always letting me know I have a place to call home, and that there is a room waiting for me if I ever need it. To my special friend Casca, thank you for opening your home to me as a safe place to do my work and making sure I took a break to eat.

And last but not least, to all the little Black girls who are not told often enough that they are pretty. I hope this book is just a subtle reminder that not only are you pretty, but you are Magic.

About the Author

~~~~~~

Yolonda Jordan first learned how to crochet from her great-aunt when she was seven years old. She has been crocheting dolls for little (and sometimes not-so-little) African American girls and boys since 2013. She released her first crochet doll pattern in 2014 and loves to see the creative spin other crocheters put on her patterns. Yolonda and her work have been featured in *Crochet World* and *Simply Crochet* magazine. She has several doll-making workshops and crochet workshops available online at myprettybrowndoll.com. Yolonda loves to travel but has made her home in rural North Carolina. She is a proud mom of two sons.

Editor: Meredith A. Clark
Designer: Jenice Kim
Design Manager: Darilyn Lowe Carnes
Managing Editor: Annalea Manalili
Production Manager: Kathleen Gaffney

Library of Congress Control Number: 2021946832

ISBN: 978-1-4197-5039-7
eISBN: 978-1-64700-106-3

Text copyright © 2022 Yolonda Jordan
Photographs copyright © 2022 Rinne Allen

Cover © 2022 Abrams

Printed and bound in China
10 9 8 7 6 5 4 3 2 1

Abrams books are available at special discounts when purchased in quantity for premiums and promotions as well as fundraising or educational use. Special editions can also be created to specification. For details, contact specialsales@abramsbooks.com or the address below.

Abrams® is a registered trademark of Harry N. Abrams, Inc.

ABRAMS The Art of Books
195 Broadway, New York, NY 10007
abramsbooks.com